OLYMPIC
GOLD

OLYMPIC GOLD

CANADA'S WINNERS IN THE SUMMER GAMES

FRANK COSENTINO
GLYNN LEYSHON

Copyright © 1975 by
Holt, Rinehart and Winston of Canada, Limited
55 Horner Avenue, Toronto, Canada M8Z 4X6

ISBN Hardbound: 0-03-923330-8
ISBN Paperbound: 0-03-923331-6
Library of Congress Catalog Card Number: 75-18456

Canadian Shared Cataloguing in Publication Data
Cosentino, Frank, 1939 –
    Olympic gold: Canadian winners of the summer games
    Frank Cosentino and Glynn Leyshon. —

Bibliography: p. 147

ISBN 0-03-923330-8.   ISBN 0-03-923331-6 pbk.

1. Olympic games.   2. Athletes – Canada.
I. Leyshon, Glynn A   1929–   II. Title.

GV721.5.C68   796.4'8   75-18456

Cover and Book Design by Carol Noel

Printed in Canada
5 4 3 2 1 79 78 77 76 75

Olympic Gold: Canada's Winners of the Summer Games is an
official history of Canadian Summer Olympic Gold Medal Winners
as authorized by The Organizing Committee of the 1976
Olympic Games.

PREFACE

Although the modern Olympics have been in existence since 1896, Canadian medallists date from the 1904 St. Louis Games where four golds were won. Representation at those early contests was in keeping with the character of the revived competitions: the financial burden was on the athlete rather than the nation he or she represented. One either had to have personal financial resources or be sponsored by an organization; there was no such thing as a "Canadian team" or an "American team", although the glory attached to Olympic victories was definitely transferred from individuals to their countries.

Canada's first official team to the Olympic Games was formed in 1908 when London was the host city. It is doubtful that the Olympics themselves were the reason for the government's interest in athletics. More than likely, it was the opportunity for the colony and its leaders to show itself off to the mother country. The Governor-General, Earl Grey, took it upon himself to commission his aide-de-camp, Hanbury-Williams, to organize a committee which would field the first representative national team.

Of course, Canadians had won honours previously. In the 1900 Games at Paris, George Orton, a Canadian competing for the United States, won a gold in the 2500 m steeplechase. In 1904, at St. Louis, the Winnipeg Shamrocks Lacrosse Club, Etienne Desmarteau, George Lyon and the Galt Association Football Club all won golds as did Billy Sherring in 1906. Although the records show that Canada won the medals, it should be noted that they were mainly the result of individual initiative and skill rather than any national program of assistance.

By 1908, however, there was a difference. A Central Olympic Committee was formed to guide Canada's fortunes. Between the Athletic Federation of Canada and the Amateur Athletic Union of Canada, two rival amateur bodies, a truce was effected; trials were held across the country and prominent sportsmen of the time, Billy Sherring and John Howard Crocker, were named coach and manager.

Eighty-four athletes were chosen to represent their country and assisted by a federal grant of $15 000 and provincial contributions totalling $5000; they returned with a total of thirteen medals. It seemed that the organization had paid off.

In 1912, Canada again followed the same pattern and although fewer than half the 1908 number of athletes was sent, a total of eight medals were earned. It was also becoming evident with the 1912 Games that other nations were arriving at the site with something more than what had previously been a cavalier attitude. Newspaper reports were beginning to pay more attention to the winners' countries than to the winners themselves.

With the interruption of the Games by the Great War, Olympianism and sport moved far from everyone's mind. In Canada, the decline and lack of enthusiasm was made painfully evident in the 1924 Summer Games where, for the first time, Canada won no golds. There was however the feeling that Canadians were capable of a better showing and once again organization and support paved the way for perhaps the height of Canada's Olympic achievements.

Prior to the 1928 Amsterdam Olympics, the Federal government contributed $26 000 to the Olympic program and a training camp lasting one month was held for the Olympic team in Hamilton. Standards for athletes had been introduced in 1926, increased in 1927 and again in 1928 in an effort to gear performance to world competition. Even the comfort of the athletes had been thought of: an advance group preceded the Olympic team to Amsterdam in those pre-Olympic village days to find suitable accommodations and look after administrative details so the athletes would have nothing to think about except competing. The preparations worked. Canada moved from 16th position in 1924 to 4th in 1928 with more than 100 points and a total of 12 medals.

In retrospect, the year 1928 appears to be the peak of Canada's sporting accomplishments in the international arena. Why? What happened to Canadian sport? What does the future hold? Certainly the lure of professional sport was making itself felt with the onset of the depression years. Whereas prior to the thirties it was generally felt that professionalism was to be avoided, the barrage of publicity surrounding and announcing the feats of those in the "big time" earning their much sought after money served to make pro sport both respectable and desirable. Football and hockey were also beginning to attract national attention, diverting the athletic focus from the international scene. Indeed, the trend has persisted to the present where athletes participating in the commercial leagues of the country are infinitely better known than their Olympic counterparts. Too, sports such as basketball persist in their refusal to play international rules within their leagues in Canada thus placing themselves at an even greater disadvantage in world competition for a reason no one seems to know.

Perhaps of even greater significance, however, has been the absence of a distinctive Canadian sporting culture. While it is very easy to place the blame for this at the doorstep of the United States

Canada's first official Olympic team, 1908. Bobby Kerr, gold medallist in the 200 m, is sitting on the last chair to the left in the front row. George Goulding, last row, second from the right, while not a winner in the 1908 Games, went on to win the gold medal for the 10 000 m walk in the next Olympiad in Stockholm.

Courtesy Marty Snellings, Toronto YMCA

and its influential presence, the fault must surely lie within Canada's own boundaries. Canadians learn of Jim Thorpe, Wilma Rudolph and Bob Mathias while being ignorant of Billy Sherring, Ethel Catherwood or Percy Williams. It has been easier for Canadians to import a mythology rather than nurture their own.

It has become evident, too, that Canadians are in effect young men and women competing against mature ones. In Canada, there is an almost total absence of club sport aside from the commercial leagues. Once performers finish high school, they may continue their athletic career at a university, but upon graduation they usually drop out of their sport, unable either to find a local club with facilities and coaching or afford the time and expenses to continue to train at the level necessary to compete internationally. The result has been that in 1972 the average age of gold medal winners was 26 for men and 28 for women, in other words, athletes at their physiological peak, while those representing Canada have generally been university students aged 21 and 22.

Against all of this, the winners of gold medals for Canada take on a special lustre. Their victories have been in spite of rather than because of any organized national system. But there is a glimmer of hope for the future. Since 1967, there has been an abundance of activity aimed at the restoration of sport as an integral part of Canadian life. Sport governing bodies have been assisted in their task; a grant sys-

tem has been devised to assist athletes and technical directors. Coaching certification schemes, Game Plan and Canada Games have all been introduced and accepted to the point that there are more topflight athletes by international standards in Canada now than ever before.

In the province of Quebec alone, concerted efforts have been made to increase its representation in the Olympics from twelve per cent in 1972 to thirty per cent in 1976 – a figure in keeping with population proportions. Its high-powered "Mission '76" seems to be right on schedule, winning the Canada Winter Games title for the first time in 1975 and in the process acting as an inspiration and a catalyst to the other provinces of the country.

But what of the Montreal Olympics and Canada's chances? Certainly a nation which has won twenty-five medals in all the summer Games will not dominate these, though there are indications that they could be among the most successful of Canada's Olympic Games in spite of the odds.

By examining the performances of other countries, it has been observed that the Olympic host country team earns one and one-half as many points in its own country's Olympics as it did in its previous performance. Hopefully, with Canada's increasing atmosphere of sports enthusiasm and support of athletes, the Canadian Olympic team will compete true to this prediction and 1976 will see Canada reaching new Olympic heights.

CONTENTS

THE BEGINNINGS

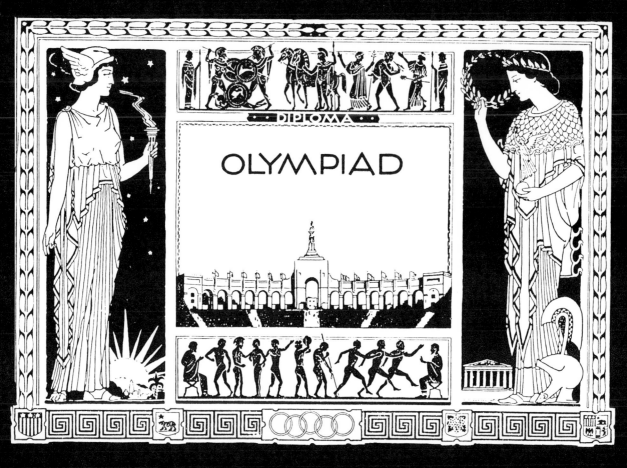

Of the many national festivals in ancient Greece, none achieved the prominence of the Games at Olympia. Chiefly religious in character, they were dedicated to Zeus: the third day of the five-day festival honouring the supreme deity of the Greek nations. Of course, in anything which extends over one thousand years, 776 BC to AD 393, changes occur. While the religious significance diminished, it is nonetheless often cited as one of the reasons the Emperor Theodosius finally banned the Games.

There were additions and deletions in the number of contests over the years, but basically the events were of the running, jumping, throwing and combative nature. Athletes competed in the nude so that women, not allowed as participants or spectators, could not disguise themselves and gain entrance.

Unquestionably the Games were a focal point for the city-states and far-flung colonies. So much so that in an area which always seemed to be at war, travellers to and from Olympia were guaranteed safe passage for a specified period before and after the Games. All were eager to see and identify with their fellow Greeks who were said to share in the divinity of Zeus as a result of an Olympic victory.

In a way, it was this Greek community of Man which Pierre de Fredy, Baron de Coubertin, was attempting to emulate in the revival of the Games. De Coubertin was greatly disheartened by the French defeat in the Franco-Prussian War of 1870. In his analysis of the two strongest nations in the world at that time, Germany and Britain, he saw that each had a core of exercise and sport as part of its educational system, especially Britain, where the sports and games of the British Public Schools caused some to say the Battle of Waterloo was won on the playing fields of Eton. De Coubertin saw sport as a way to channel the emotions of nationalism towards an international arena, where competition could take place on the athletic rather than the battlefield.

Of course, that is not to say that de Coubertin's aspirations were all realized but the time for his ideas had definitely come. In the ancient Games, only a privileged class, freeborn male Greeks, was allowed to participate, and continuing in the nineteenth century, it was declared that only "amateurs", the privileged group of that time, would be eligible.

It was a consistent decision. From almost the beginning of civilization, sport was the province of the "haves" of a society. Until the Industrial Revolution, average people were too occupied trying to eke out a living working from sunrise to sunset and simply did not have the time to divert their attention to sport. Once, however, time became available to the working class, the water-taxi operator was free to compete with the gentleman (amateur) rower, the footman with the gentleman (amateur) runner and so on into every sport which had previously been barred to them. There developed the definite problem that social "inferiors" were entering competions with their "bet-

Pierre de Frédy, Baron de Coubertin, the founder of the modern Olympics.

ters". The latter were mainly interested in the competition as a social exercise between people of like backgrounds; the former – simply in finding out who was really the best.

To keep things "fair", it was ruled that those who were engaged in any form of manual labour were to be excluded from sports competition since it was felt their occupation gave them a strength advantage over the upper classes who, if they worked at all, did so in a sedentary manner. As a result, one of the first amateur codes was that of the Henley Regatta in England which ruled that one could not be an amateur if one had ever been, by trade or employment, an artisan, mechanic or labourer; a regulation which, incidentally, was in effect for the 1908 Games in London.

To many, however, while they agreed with the sentiment, the regulation as stated was too blunt and offensive. A way around the obvious class discrimination was found when it was reasoned that since the working class were the ones to be restricted and since those same people earned money in their work, anyone who earned money in sports or sports-related work, could not be classified as an amateur. When one looks at the aristocrats who were attracted to the Olympic movement in its formative stages, there is no question that the limiting of entrants to the "amateur class" was based on the above logic and therefore a reason for the Games' initial acceptance and growth.

Yet it should not be assumed that

they were an automatic success. When the revived Games were offered to Athens, the government balked when costs of staging them became known. Outside of a postage stamp issued to commemorate the event, the money was raised privately; one Greek businessman, George Averoff of Alexandria, built a stadium along ancient lines complete with marble seats and a standing room capacity of 60 000.

Perhaps the greatest impetus to the Games was the idea of Michel Breal who suggested that a marathon race, in commemoration of the famous run of Pheidippides during the Persian War, should be included in the revived Games. The ancient Greeks might have recoiled in horror at the brazen disregard

of their motto "nothing in excess", but Breal's idea was enthusiastically accepted, although the distance of 26 miles, 385 yards was not finalized until the 1908 Games.

To be sure, there were growing pains. The initial 1896 Games were attended by only twelve nations; there was very little publicity outside of Greece and the nations were represented by private clubs or individuals who both could afford to go and had heard of the Olympic contests. In its early naivete, the competitions were thought of as between players from different countries rather than as nation against nation, way of life versus way of life. With the exception of the Games in Greece, it was not until the 1912 Olympics that they

March past of the Canadian athletes at the 1908 London Games.

Courtesy Greek National Tourist Office

The original Olympic stadium in Olympia, Greece, where the first ancient Games were held. The length of the stadium, about 560 feet, was said to be the distance Hercules could walk while holding his breath.

achieved some prominence as an event in themselves.

The Olympics of 1900, 1904 and 1908 were each held as an adjunct to an exposition and while the 1908 Games did have some individual stature, the 1900 events stretched out over a period of five months without even the word Olympic in their official title! The 1904 St. Louis Games, while they were officially called Olympics, nonetheless stretched out over another five-month period during the Louisiana Purchase Exposition. The 1912 Olympic Games, the last before the Great War, seemed to signal the growth of the movement and, at the same time, marked the decline of the traditional ways. War would eliminate many Victorian ideas: the period following would be one of more growth and symbolism, marching with the spirit of the times.

1904
Lacrosse
The Winnipeg Shamrocks
Canada's First Gold Medal

It was as if a bombshell had hit. Lacrosse was going to be an event at the Olympic Games! Not only that, but the Games were going to be in St. Louis, within easy travelling distance. The previous Olympics – the 1896 Games in Athens and the 1900 Games in Paris – had been too far away. True, George Orton of Toronto had won a gold medal in 1900 in the 2500 m steeplechase, but he was attending the University of Pennsylvania, and competed for the United States. Now, not only would Canadians have a chance to enter the Olympics, they could do so in the "national game".

Plans for the 1904 Olympics were confused right from the day of the first announcement that the Games would be held in the United States. With the American success at Athens and Paris, it was only natural that the Games be awarded to the world's gold mine of sport. Both Chicago and St. Louis vied for the honour of hosting the event, and it wasn't until early in 1904 that St. Louis was finally awarded the Games as an adjunct to the Louisiana Purchase Exposition, with sporting competitions spread out between July and November.

To lessen travelling expenses for the Europeans, the Americans agreed to send a boat to a European Capital and bring all the national teams to the Games. But no boat materialized and "Meet Me in St. Louis" became more than just a popular song written to publicize the fair – it seemed to be a sardonic message for the Europeans waiting to be met in Europe. As a result, only a handful of representatives from European nations arrived.

Lacrosse suffered less from lack of European competition than did most events. It was the game of the New World. To the Canadians there was almost a missionary zeal about its benefits. From the days when it was played by the Indians and known as *baggattaway*, and then "refined" for the white man by the Montreal dentist George Beers, it was *the* Canadian game. In the midst of the joy at the prospect of having lacrosse in the Olympics, a snag developed. Only amateurs could compete in the Games, and while no one seemed to be absolutely sure of what an amateur was, it was well established by this time that he couldn't be an athlete who earned money from his sport. The lacrosse world was thrown into a tizzy.

In an effort to provide "baseball management" for lacrosse, the National Lacrosse Union had closed its eyes while clubs offered inducements to players. Money and jobs were used to bind a player to a club, insure his coming to practice, and develop the team's skills to attract the paying public. In the process, the league continually ran afoul of the Canadian Amateur Athletic Union: almost every player in the League was declared a professional in 1904 for having accepted money or for playing with or against someone who had been declared a professional.

The Winnipeg Lacrosse Club, though not involved in the Olympic competition, played an exhibition match against the Winnipeg Shamrocks to raise money for the trip to St. Louis.

Out of the confusion emerged the green-shirted Shamrocks of Winnipeg; they were the champions of Western Canada and the United States and, more importantly, they were in good standing with the amateur authorities. The Shamrocks would go to St. Louis. It was the first time that a Manitoba team would leave the province to compete for a championship of this type, and its importance was not lost on the public.

The Shamrocks had been in existence for only three years, but during that time they had attracted the support of many followers. They had lost only on four occasions and the fans enjoyed their spirited play. Everyone was going to contribute to the travel fund. The Maroons offered to play a benefit baseball game; both the Mintos and the Winnipeg Lacrosse Club offered to

Manitoba Archives

play contests against the Shamrocks with any surplus raised to be directed towards the Shamrocks' expenses.

On June 28 at Fort Garry Park, the "Shams" were given their first test. They passed it with flying colours, defeating the Minto Lacrosse Club by a 12–2 score. While the play of the champions was a source of joy, the attendance was not. Fewer than five hundred saw the exhibition. Civic pride seemed to be stung by the report. For the next game, against the Winnipeg Lacrosse Club, a "tremendous" crowd of three thousand watched the "fastest lacrosse game ever seen in Winnipeg". Everybody was pleased. The immense crowd had contributed heavily to the fund, a good game had been seen, and the Shamrocks had won 5–4. Amid great excitement, the Shamrocks left the next day for St. Paul, Minnesota, en route to Chicago and St. Louis.

The Shamrock boys stopped over in St. Paul and played an exhibition game against the champions of the city. American newspapers described the meeting as the "greatest game ever played in St. Paul". Some twenty-five hundred fans attended the game at Lexington Park and cheered the locals on to unexpected heights. Manitobans, however, didn't know whether to be more upset with the result – a 6–6 tie – or the fact that the game was played on a Sunday!

The Chicago Calumets were entered in the lacrosse tourney as well, and had invited the "green-shirted men from the north" to play

a preliminary game. Before a large crowd of two thousand at Chicago's National Ball Park, the Canadians put on a dazzling display of passing and teamwork while scoring fifteen goals to Chicago's five. The Calumets had entertained high hopes of winning the Olympic Games competition but having played the northerners thought better of it and withdrew from the competition.

People today, accustomed to the grandiose sites of recent Olympiads, would probably be disappointed with the site of 1904. The Fair buildings and exhibits were marvels to behold; beautiful pavilions housed the exhibits which glorified the future, but the athletic facilities seemed to have been constructed as an afterthought. The traditional ceremonies associated with the Games were non-existent; the only hint that the facilities were associated with the Olympics was that they were located at the northeastern corner of the Fair Grounds along an avenue appropriately named "Olympian Way".

No matter. The Shamrocks were in St. Louis, these were the Olympic Games, and the winners would be a part of recorded history! Four teams were entered in the quest for the championship honours: Winnipeg, the Mohawk Athletic Club, the Brooklyn Crescents and the St. Louis Amateur Athletic Association. St. Louis was paired with the Mohawk Indians the Crescents with the Shamrocks. But the Brooklyn team was nowhere to be found! The Shamrocks were given the bye, and officials hastily decided that

the winners of the St. Louis-Mohawk game would play the Canadians in a two-game series for the title and the Olympic gold medal.

The Shamrocks were quite an imposing sight when they took the field against the Triple A's from St. Louis. Cloutier, Flett, Laidlaw, Pentland, Orris, Cattanach, Bretz, Down, Jamieson, Blanchard, Brennough, Burns and Lyle put on a pre-game display of passing and catching which seemed to rattle the locals. In a contest highlighted by the confident play of the Canadians, the home side was outscored 6–1. The Shamrocks were halfway to the gold.

The second game of the series turned out to be a much closer one. At the end of the third quarter Winnipeg was leading 3–2; it was plain to see that the Americans were having problems. They had difficulty penetrating the defense of the Canadian side, finally resorting to long shots which were easily handled. On the other hand, the Canucks were able to scoop loose balls from the ground, pass quickly so as to isolate two on one, and take shots from close in. Their superiority began to tell in the fourth quarter, when much to the delight of the small Canadian contingent – tourists and exhibit staff members – the green power broke loose; five unanswered goals were tallied. The game was won 8–2; the series 14–3.

It was a happy group of athletes who wandered about the Fair Grounds that night. Each player

The Shamrock Boys are corkers.
They're not the kind that's slow,
They're born and bred lacrossers,
As we would have you know.
You may talk about your Winnipegs,
The Chicago boys as well,
But they can't compare with the Shamrock Boys,
The Shamrock Boys so swell.

had been awarded a gold locket and the team was presented with a huge silver banner to be inscribed with each player's name. No matter what exhibit they wandered into, someone would recognize them and offer congratulations. Their visit to the "Irish Village" on the Pike was the signal for more backslapping, singing and toasts to Canada and the "old sod".

On the way home, the Chicago Calumets hosted the Olympic champions to a gala reception, which provided a debut for the instant composing-singing trio of Carper, Laidlaw and Lyle! In their finest voice, the trio of tenors raised their glasses and sang a boisterous rendition of "The Shamrock Boys".

It was a gala celebration, one which was still the talk of "The Shamrock Boys" as their train pulled into the station at St. Paul, Minnesota, for another exhibition game. The Shamrocks had only one request. The game couldn't be played on a Sunday. A Saturday game it was, with the Shamrocks taking the contest 7–5.

Back in Winnipeg, a great celebration was in store. Bands played, people cheered and speeches were made in honour of the conquering heroes. Nothing was too good for these young men. Not only had they shown St. Paul the error of their ways in scheduling Sunday games, the Shamrock Boys had also won Canada's first gold medal in the Olympic Games, and Winnipeg was very proud indeed!

1904
56·Pound
Weight Throw
Etienne
Desmarteau
Mr. Hammer

In the first week of September, 1904, the police constables of Montreal's Station Number Five were stringing bunting and decorating their station house to welcome back their fellow officer, Etienne Desmarteau. Two weeks earlier he would not have been welcome at all. He had been fired for disobeying his superiors' orders and taking time off work to compete in the St. Louis Olympics.

But Desmarteau had just won a gold medal, and in the midst of the preparations for his reception, the

Police Department conveniently "lost" his dismissal notice.

Before going to the Olympics in St. Louis, Etienne had spent several years competing and practising at his specialty – the 56-pound weight throw. The weight in this case was actually a large paving stone. Its awkward size made it unpopular, and by the 1920's the 56-pound weight throw became as outdated as the dinosaur.

But in the first few years of the new century, Etienne and his brothers, especially Zachary, practised diligently at the event and travelled widely seeking competition. They represented the Montreal Police Athletic Association in the years prior to the Olympic Games in St. Louis.

It was while competing for the MPAA in Ottawa early in August 1904, that Etienne compiled a remarkable record. He and brother Zachary had entered all the throwing events in the meet and in practically every case they finished first and second respectively. The results of the eighth annual tournament of the Ottawa Police AA in Lansdowne Park, Ottawa, show Etienne winning the 16-pound hammer throw with a distance of 138 feet, the discus with a distance of 106 feet, the 16-pound shot-put with 39 feet, 8.5 inches and the 56-

Constable Desmarteau before he was fired from the Montreal Police Force for defying his superiors and competing in the Olympics. His dismissal notice was mysteriously "lost" after he won a gold medal.

Authors' Collection

pound weight throw with a Canadian record of 36 feet, 6.5 inches.

To add to his accomplishments, Etienne then entered and won the throw for height, setting another Canadian record. He threw the 56-pound weight 14 feet, 8 inches straight up! In all, Etienne finished the day with five firsts including two records, while Zachary had two seconds and a third.

Perhaps Etienne had felt the sting of John Flanagan's prodigious heave of the 56-pound weight earlier in the summer. Flanagan, like Etienne, was a policeman, but from New York where he enjoyed advantages in terms of coaching and travelling expenses. In July of 1904 he set a world record, throwing the 56-pound weight 40 feet, 2 inches. He did this, however, with "unlimited run and follow". At the Olympics, all weight throwers would be required to stay within a nine-foot ring.

"Genial" John Flanagan was a redoubtable opponent. In 1902 Desmarteau had defeated him at the New York AAU championships and Flanagan, for all his easy-going ways, was anxious to avenge that defeat. He avidly hoped for a chance to compete against Desmarteau in the first Olympics to be held on the North American continent. Flanagan's new world record made him more determined than

Etienne Desmarteau with his Montreal Police Athletic Association T-shirt and one of his namesakes—a competition throwing hammer.

ever to match strength with the Montreal policeman.

The Desmarteaus were a long-established French-Canadian family. Interestingly enough, the original family name was Birtz and the first of the lineage settled in Boucherville Quebec in 1757. The Etienne Birtz who started the line was said to possess herculean strength and in the tradition of strong men was a blacksmith.

His shop had a sign consisting of two crossed hammers which earned him the nickname Des Marteaux. This nickname, with the final "x" missing, ultimately became the family name. Thus, Etienne Desmarteau of 1904 had a tradition of strength going back 150 years.

Etienne himself was hardly the giant of legend. He was a quiet, modest man who stood 6 feet tall and weighed 208 pounds at his prime. He was just 31 years old when he won his gold medal and almost exactly a year later he was to die of typhoid fever. But at the time of the Olympics he was in peak condition and had several years of preparation behind him. He won the Canadian Championship in the 56-pound weight throw in 1902, 1903, and 1904. He burned to go to St. Louis.

The brass of the Montreal Police were reluctant to give Etienne time off work to pursue such a frivolous pastime as weight throwing. In addition, the Montreal Police Athletic Association refused to sponsor Desmarteau's trip.

Etienne was quite willing to take a leave without pay to go to St. Louis but the administration would

not hear of it, although his immediate superior, Captain Loye, recommended that Desmarteau be allowed to go.

Finally the Montreal Amateur Athletic Association agreed to underwrite part of his trip, but Etienne went into competition wearing the colours of the Palestra Nationale of Montreal.

The heat in St. Louis was heavy and constant and interfered with the great Flanagan. He voiced his concern over whether or not he could handle his old rival. He complained of mild sickness. Etienne, on the other hand, was fit and strong. He had resigned his job on the police force and made his way down to St. Louis as best he could. He practised daily with some of the other Canadians who, sponsored as Etienne was by individual clubs, wore club uniforms rather than Canadian colours into competition. It made it difficult to tell which country a man represented.

The day of the competition dawned bright and hot. At the stadium, Flanagan was heard to complain about the heat and even Etienne did not feel at his best. All the athletes were acquainted with the handicap system which would be used. In the handicap, the difference between the best and the worst competitors was almost eliminated. Thus Johnson of the USA had an advantage of 11 feet while Desmarteau had one of only 6 inches In other words, Johnson would have 11 feet added to his best effort while Desmarteau would have only 6 inches added to his. Fortunately, this was only done for

purposes of competition and not for the record. Newspapers of the day, however, carried the name of Johnson as the winner since his handicap gave him first place.

The competition began with the giant Californian, Rose, taking the first throw. He managed only to foul, not being familiar with the rule requiring him to stay in the nine-foot ring. His best throw finally was 28 feet.

Next, Etienne Desmarteau stepped into the circle. Using his favourite method of taking just one turn before launching the weight, he managed an impressive toss of 34 feet, 4 inches.

The great Flanagan was next and he looked worried. Putting all his strength behind his throw, Flanagan managed 33 feet, 4 inches, a foot less than Desmarteau. Jim Mitchell, another US strong man, made his attempt and was only one inch short of Flanagan's mark.

Desmarteau, Flanagan and Mitchell qualified for the final along with yet another American, Henneman. Fatigue and heat took their toll. Despite their best efforts, none of the finalists could better their marks made in the preliminaries. Under the rules, the best recorded throw of the day was registered for each man regardless of whether the throw was made in the first or second round. Etienne Desmarteau had won an Olympic gold medal! To their credit, the Americans cheered him as a champion. They hoisted "Frenchy" on their shoulders and toured him around to the great delight of Desmarteau's

Montreal teammates.

It was the custom of the times to award something more than merely a gold medal. In this case, Mr. D. R. Francis, president of the St. Louis Exposition, awarded Etienne Desmarteau a handsome cup worth $250 in addition to the medal.

The newspapers, whose writers were understandably puzzled by some of the publicity given to the Olympics published somewhat conflicting reports of the event. *The Globe* of September 2, 1904, listed Johnson of the US as first with a throw of 25 feet, 8 inches, while Desmarteau was listed as fourth. *The Montreal Star,* however, gave an enlightened version as the official report, ranking Desmarteau as fourth but also giving his actual winning throw.

The story of Etienne Desmarteau faded quickly from the Canadian scene. In 1911 a reference was made to him in the Annual General Meeting of the AAU of Canada. A certain Duncan Gillis, a hammer thrower, was praised as being on a par with the great Desmarteau. Gillis placed second in the hammer throw in the 1912 Olympics just missing the greatness predicted for him.

As for Etienne, his name and his performance virtually disappeared until 1955 when he was installed as a member of Canada's Sports Hall of Fame in Toronto. The throwing of the 56-pound weight was discontinued after the 1904 Olympics, revived for one brief appearance in the 1920 Olympics and then was dropped, never to surface again.

In 1904, golf was included in the Olympic competitions. This event was just one highlight in the career of the remarkable golfer from Toronto's Lambton Club – George S. Lyon, Canada's most unique athlete.

Lyon, it seemed, could do anything. In 1876, at the age of eighteen, he set a Canadian pole vault record. Then, interrupting his promising athletic development, he joined the Queen's Own Rifles and served as a sergeant during the North West Rebellion.

When he returned to Toronto he became the captain and second baseman of the city championship baseball team in 1886 and 1887, and at the same time, a top tennis player. His natural ability in bat and racquet sports, led him to cricket and, not surprisingly, he became an outstanding player, batting 238 not out; a Canadian record which remained unbroken for many years.

Today, George Lyon is remembered primarily as a first-rate golfer; yet, before his thirty-eighth birthday he had never swung a golf club! Typical of his confidence and sense of challenge, he took up golf on a dare.

The Rosedale Cricket grounds and golf course were separated from each other only by a fence. In October 1896, while Lyon was playing cricket, a friend, John Dick, was playing through on the adjoining golf course. Dick spotted Lyon and made a remark about using such a big bat to hit the ball. Lyon accepted his dare to come over and see if he could hit the golf ball with

1904 Golf
George Seymour Lyon
The Man Who Golfed On A Dare

the club and a whole new career was started. Lyon literally climbed the fence into a new career. He continued to play cricket but his new love was golf and he pursued it with a passion.

Having learned the game at such a late stage in his life, it was only natural that the novice would incorporate his baseball and cricket swing in his new sport. His style, or rather his lack of it, was once described by a New York critic as being akin to "using a scythe to cut wheat". But only one year after he was dared to try the game, Lyon was considered to be the best golfer at Rosedale, in spite of his form which continued to amuse unknowing bystanders.

One of his earliest tournaments was during that first year after his "conversion" when Rosedale competed against the Toronto Golf Club team in an inter-club match. Lyon was matched against Toronto's best golfer, Bethune. Lyon's teammates warned him not to be disappointed or downhearted with a loss, because Bethune not only had golfed for many years but he could make the golf ball do almost anything he wanted. It was a surprised group of spectators that watched the "reaper" give the Toronto golfer a neat trimming.

If Lyon ever needed any incentive, his win over Bethune must have provided it. Shortly before his fortieth birthday he decided to enter the Canadian Amateur championship. Lyon surprised everybody by winning twelve up. For someone who had played golf for only two years it was an amazing feat. He

had proven himself to his club mates and was asked to play in the first international golf match between Canada and the United States on October 1, 1898.

To those who didn't know him, George Lyon looked anything like a top golfer. He was a portly man who loved to joke, and played with a boisterous enthusiasm. He had an aggressive cheerfulness about him and always seemed to be singing songs like "My Wild Irish Rose", or walking about on his hands. Other golfers shook their heads in disbelief when he took what appeared to be a haphazard and ruthless swipe at the ball and knocked it far down the fairway, invariably in the right direction. Despite his adapted cricket swing, Lyon won the Canadian title in 1900 and 1903. In 1904, Lyon and two Hamilton mates, A. E. Austin and his sixteen-year-old son Bertie, decided to enter the Olympic Golf competitions in St. Louis. Eighty-four golfers from North America and Europe entered in the hope of winning what some were already calling a world championship, scheduled to begin Monday, September 18, 1904.

Rains had fallen during Saturday and Sunday, leaving the grounds at the Glen Echo Club of St. Louis so soft that in some cases balls sunk a half-inch into the ground after the drive. By noon Monday the rain had stopped and the course became drier and faster. At the end of the qualifying round, the eighty-four hopefuls were pared to thirty-two. Chandler Egan, an American, led the pack with 163 while Lyon was in ninth place with 169.

Lyon had raised some eyebrows with his style of play in the first round but he was never considered a threat. The second round was to provide some indication of his future in the tournament – he was devastating. It was as if he had overheard some of the comments circulating about his style. He played like a dynamo and set a course record by defeating the hometown favourite by eleven holes with nine to play.

Eight players were left in the search for gold and the third round: three from St. Louis, three from Chicago, one from Seattle, and Lyon.

St. Louis papers had taken to berating the Canadian for his terrible form. Sure, they said, he drove the ball great distances, but that hardly made it golf! Nonetheless, Lyon defeated his third-round opponent by four strokes and won himself a place in the semifinal.

The fourth round match between Lyon and Newton, the Pacific Coast champion, was called the best game of the competition. The eighth and ninth holes were described as "being negotiated by the cleverest golf ever seen in North America", the highlight being a drive of 327 yards by Lyon.

To all appearances, the final for the 1904 Olympic gold medal seemed a mismatch. On the one hand, there was the youthful Chandler Egan, the twenty-three-year-old wonder, recently crowned as champion of the United States. He was an excellent driver, a clutch putter and had demonstrated

Courtesy Fred Lyon

THE GLEN ECHO CUP

his superiority throughout the week by winning all of his matches with relative ease. He was clearly the favourite.

His opponent, George Seymour Lyon, was not taken seriously. As a forty-six-year-old, rather dumpy-looking man, he just didn't *look* like he stood a chance – a feeling

which was reinforced every time he took a swipe at the unfortunate ball. He appeared to put up a brave front with his endless stream of alternating singing and chatter but many felt that was like whistling past a graveyard. Then too, there was the story circulating that the veteran had suffered a severe attack of hay fever and wasn't able to golf much during the summer. Coupled with the long train trip from Toronto and the mental and physical pressures of four tough rounds of golf against some of the best competition in the world, the general feeling was the middle-aged upstart was on the verge of collapse.

No one knew better than Lyon that he was the underdog. Nobody knew, however, how he was seething inwardly. Newspapers, referring to his "Coal-heaver's swing" prompted him to write to the Secretary of the United States Golf Association; nothing elaborate or flowery, just a simple statement: "Whether I play like a sailor or a coal-heaver, I never said that I am proud of my form. I only do the best I can".

As game day approached, he looked more of an underdog. The skies had opened up and rain was falling heavily. Yet Lyon was enthusiastic as he stepped up to the first hole amid polite applause from the large gallery there to watch his expected defeat. With a swat developed from his many years of cricket, Lyon drove to within eight yards of the 276 yard first hole. Two putts and he was in; one up on Egan. At the end of eighteen and the noon break, Lyon was still one up.

At three o'clock, the two finalists started out in the last eighteen. The gallery swelled. A host of eager onlookers were anxious to see the climax of the match that was the talk of the clubhouse. The nineteenth was even but at the twentieth and twenty-first, Egan's game developed a hitch. His drives were errant. Traps, long grasses, hazards, all sorts of obstacles seemed to be attracting his ball. Meanwhile, Lyon's play remained steady; he was three up after twenty-two; four up after twenty-four.

Much to the delight of the huge throng, however, Egan began regaining his championship form and won the next two holes. On the thirtieth, when it appeared that

Lyon would be forced to two putt and lose another hole, he sank a long ten-footer to retain his two hole lead. But Egan maintained his momentum to win the thirty-first, cutting Lyon's lead to one. On the thirty-third, Lyon drove down the middle of the fairway. A groan went up from the partisan crowd as Egan's drive ended up in the lake. He was having his problems again. Lyon slapped, coaxed and patted his ball into the hole to win it and go two up with three to play.

The thirty-fourth was almost a replay of the thirty-third, with Lyon winning the hole to go three up with two to play and end the "greatest golf tournament ever held in America".

In his characteristic style, George Lyon accepted his prizes after

walking on his hands through the path the onlookers had cleared for him at the clubhouse. It was an uproarious ceremony. Lyon showed no effects of the long pressure-packed week of golf. By the end of the evening, all were singing Lyon's favourite song, "My Wild Irish Rose", at the tops of their voices.

Many felt that Lyon had reached the apex of his career and yet, as it turned out it seemed to be only the beginning. His Olympic victory launched him to even greater heights. He won the Canadian title in 1905, 1906, 1907, 1912, and 1914. During the war, he and his friend Chick Evans, played a series of exhibition matches, raising thirty thousand dollars for the war effort in the process.

At the end of the Great War, Lyon was sixty years old and turned to Senior Championships, winning titles every year from 1918 to 1930 with the exception of 1924, 1927 and 1929. He probably would have won in 1929 as well but after making it to the finals, he withdrew. His son was getting married the same afternoon and for Lyon, attending the wedding was more important than winning the championship at the Royal Ottawa course.

Lyon had the opportunity to become the first Canadian to win two gold medals at the Olympics. In 1908, at the London Games, golf was included again on the Olympic program. He made the trip to London and prepared himself for the defense of his title. As the deadline for entries arrived and passed, Lyon's was judged the only

one acceptable. A dispute among the UK golfers caused the golfers of that country to boycott the Olympics and Americans simply didn't want to make the long trip with all the uncertainty. When the Games Committee told Lyon that he would be awarded the gold medal by default, Lyon refused to accept it. He wanted no part of a medal he hadn't won in a fair competition!

When Lyon turned seventy in 1928, he was still golfing competitively, still winning championships, and determined to shoot his age at least once a year over eighteen holes. He succeeded every year until his seventy-ninth birthday when a broken wrist prevented him from reaching his goal. Perhaps ''Providence was thus foretelling that his seventy-nine and seventy-ninth year was the end of the trail''. After a winter's illness, he died in his eightieth year.

George S. Lyon remains one of the most remarkable athletes in Canada's history. His contributions in so many fields were recognized in 1967 by the Ontario Golf Association and in 1971 by the Royal Canadian Golf Association Hall of Fame. His spirit of competition and fair play are recalled each year at the Lambton Club with the opening and closing of the golf season. At his former golf club and at some point during the awards dinner of the Canadian Seniors championship, Lyon's favourite song ''My Wild Irish Rose'' is joyfully sung – a fitting tribute to a great Canadian athlete whose motto was: ''I only do my best''.

Courtesy Fred Lyon

1904 Soccer

The Galt Association Football Club

The Canadian "Champions of America"

It was the biggest night in Galt's history. Excitement was in the air. The light from the flickering torches was causing shadows to dance. No one seemed to notice the slight chill in the air. The people of Galt had come out 2500 strong, filling the railroad station and spilling outside, along, and beyond the long passenger platform. It was Monday night, November 21, 1904, and the Galt Football Club, 1904 Olympic Gold Medallists, were coming home.

None should have been surprised, but when the announcement was posted on the giant newsboard at the *Galt Weekly Reformer* offices, Galt became ecstatic. The little community was proud of its team — all local boys and products of the best Football Association in Canada.

Those were confusing days for football in Canada. The Grey Cup had not yet been presented, and Canadian football was still closely aligned to rugby with fourteen-men teams. The ball was put into play by being "heeled out" by the "centre scrimmage". It was mostly played in the larger centres and universities. The "association game" was just beginning to be known by the faddish name of "soccer" and had caught on in the smaller communities where there were sizable British concentrations — notably the central Ontario towns of Galt (Cambridge) and Berlin (Kitchener), and the large British settlements in Manitoba and British Columbia.

But in this, the twenty-fifth anniversary year of the Galt Football Club, it was more evident than ever that Galt was the football capital of the new world — "the

Manchester of Canada". The club had a unique history. Forty championships of all sorts were won during that quarter century. Just five years after its formation, it made a successful trip to St. Louis to be the first Canadian team to participate in an international soccer competition. It repeated its successes at the Chicago World's Fair in 1893. In 1903 the club toured Manitoba playing seventeen games — winning sixteen and tying one. It was a 3500 mile trip and club officials loved to remind everyone not only of their success on the field but also of the fact that gate receipts covered all expenses except one hundred dollars. The word around the league was that "the club management is composed of shrewd and able financiers who always manage to have a snug balance in the treasury".

The road to the Olympics was a familiar story for all the townspeople. For a time it seemed as if there might be three Canadian representatives going to St. Louis. The Berlin Rangers and the University of Toronto were each interested but as the time approached for the mid-November competitions, only Galt remained.

First Berlin decided to drop out. There was some talk about their concern over the players' amateur status, but this was later denied by

This is the medal presented to Fred Steep, the team's right forward, by Galt's Mayor Mundy. Similar medals were given to each player in a ceremony at the Canadian exhibit.

23

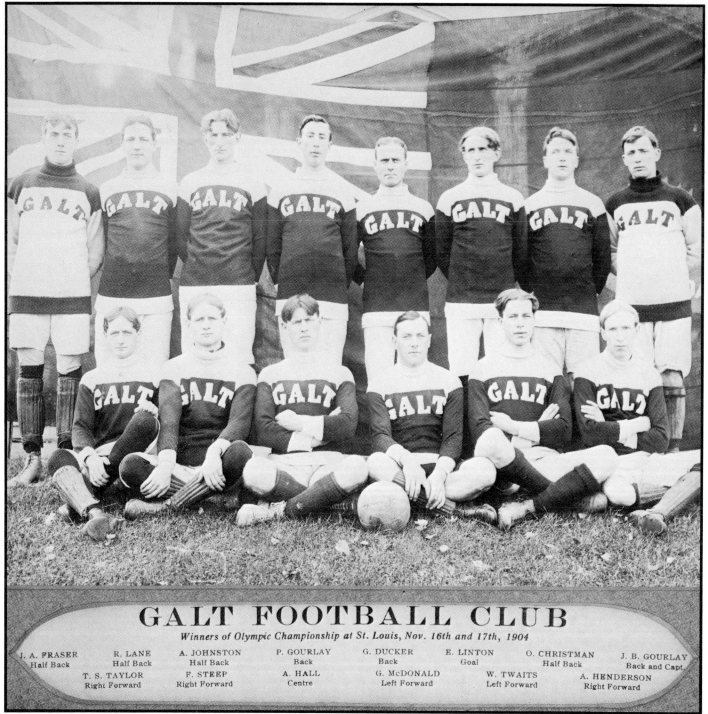

GALT FOOTBALL CLUB

Winners of Olympic Championship at St. Louis, Nov. 16th and 17th, 1904

| J. A. FRASER | R. LANE | A. JOHNSTON | P. GOURLAY | G. DUCKER | E. LINTON | O. CHRISTMAN | J. B. GOURLAY |
| Half Back | Half Back | Half Back | Back | Back | Goal | Half Back | Back and Capt. |

| T. S. TAYLOR | F. STEEP | A. HALL | G. McDONALD | W. TWAITS | A. HENDERSON |
| Right Forward | Right Forward | Centre | Left Forward | Left Forward | Right Forward |

club management. And it wasn't, they insisted, that they couldn't beat the Galt team. They simply couldn't afford the five hundred dollars the trip would cost.

The University of Toronto? Well there was a story. There was a lot of jubilation in Galt after the game in Toronto on November 5. The Galt boys taught them a lesson about football, shattering them with a 2–0 score. Up until then the University team was all set to travel to St. Louis; but there was no sense in going if they couldn't beat Galt.

If there was any wailing in Berlin or Toronto, there certainly wasn't evidence of anything but spirited anticipation in Galt. A "smoker" was held in the Town Hall to wind up the season and prepare for the St. Louis trip. The applause seemed to get louder and more unrestrained as the evening went on. Each player was introduced; each was enthusiastically cheered. These were local boys, well-known to all: John Gourlay – the captain – and his brother, George Ducker, Ernest Linton, Otto Christman, Albert Johnston, John Fraser, Robert Lane, Fred Steep, Gordon McDonald, Alex Hall, William Twaits, Albert Henderson, and Tom Taylor. The cheer that greeted Tom Taylor – perhaps the fastest outside right player the team ever

On the Friday morning following their gold medal victory, the Galt Association Football Club posed for this photograph with the 1904 Olympics' officials. Behind them is the Canadian Building – part of the Louisiana Purchase Exposition.

had – almost brought the house down.

The Grand Trunk Railway announced that it would offer special rates of $10.70 return to St. Louis. A special car would be set aside for the team and its supporters! Fifty people including mayor Mundy were in the party.

Even the entire train was special – red and white streamers throughout the car, red and white fan-shaped decorations under the windows, flags flying from the rear, and a huge sign letting everybody know that it was the Galt Football Club passing through on its way to the great Fair.

By four o'clock on the afternoon of the game, people started gathering outside the *Galt Weekly Reformer* offices, waiting for the news. When the 7–0 score was posted, Galt went wild.

The Christian Brothers' College team was no match for the Canadians. After a scoreless twenty minutes with each team feeling the other out, Galt erupted for four goals in the last ten minutes of the first half, and three more in the second half. McDonald and Steep each scored two goals with Taylor scoring the remaining one. The pride of the townspeople was written all over their faces as they read the dispatches from the St. Louis papers about the clean and tactical play of the northerners. While most American teams preferred long shots at the goal, the Canadians played with short passes and dribbled the ball almost to the goal mouth with the goalie at their mercy.

Thursday, an even larger crowd

was gathered at the newsboard. The St. Rose team of St. Louis was supposed to be much stronger than the Christian Brothers' College team. As the 4–0 score was posted, a deafening cheer started from the front of the crowd and roared its way to the back.

The first half of the game had been scoreless, but after a chalk talk by team captain John Gourlay, and a sensational exhibition by Tom Taylor with two goals, the Galt team brought Canada its fourth gold medal of the Olympic Games.

The team was invited to a formal reception by Commissioner Hutchinson at the Canadian exhibit where Mayor Mundy presented each member of the team with a gold medal emblematic of their Olympic victory. Even a photograph had been arranged for Friday morning in front of the Canadian exhibit! There was just time for a quick tour of the Fair grounds before the team left for Chicago and an exhibition game against the Wanderers. Fifteen hundred people, half of them Canadians, watched some spectacular plays as the Olympic champions defeated the Chicago side 4–2. Even the Chicago paper stated that Galt had demonstrated the right to be called "Champions of America"!

The wailing whistle of the Grand Trunk engine was the first indication that the boys were home. Off in the distance could be heard the puffing of the train as it neared the end of its long journey. People craned their necks to see if they could spot the headlight. Little boys

climbed fences and trees to get a better vantage point. Whistles and bells started pealing forth their congratulatory welcomes. As the train huffed into sight a mighty cheer drowned out the hissing engine. The cheer grew even louder when Captain John Gourlay led each of the players off the train as the band struck up "Hail the Conquering Hero's Come"!

What a night! The only thing that even rivalled it was the day back in '01 when all of Galt's Association Football teams, the Juniors, Intermediates and Seniors had won Canadian Championships. Over at the Opera House where the team was due for an informal reception, every seat had been taken up by eight o'clock.

The torchbearers moved to the front of the station. Carriages, bands, autos, bicycles, townspeople young and old all fell in behind for the march through town to the Opera House. The players occupied the place of honour. The Opera House was proudly decorated in red and white. A continuous din was punctuated with a loud and sustained burst of applause as the official party made its way onto the stage. There could be no attempt made to be overly formal. That would come later in the week.

All agreed that Galt had never

Association Football got its name from the game's British controlling body – the National Football Association. Today the game is called soccer, a word derived from a slang alteration of "association".

Courtesy Orville Steep

27

been so enthusiastic about anything. The decision was wisely made to adjourn after the introduction of the players and Mayor Mundy's remarks. The cheers were interspersed with the sound of the breaking of windows and doors by those trying to get in. Scott's Opera House just wasn't built for that type of enthusiasm!

The formal reception was held at the Opera House on November 30, 1904 and the Galt Weekly *Reformer* of December 1, 1904 covered it this way:

The formal and official reception to the Galt Football team, winners of the Olympic Championship at St. Louis was held in the Opera House last night and was attended by an immense audience of admirers.

Acting Mayor Fryer was chairman. He opened the reception by reading an address of welcome to the team which he subsequently handed over to the keeping of Captain John B. Gourlay.

Following the reading of the address, each member of the team was presented with a handsome watch fob and as each man advanced, he was given a rousing reception to which he bowed his acknowledgement.

The Address of Welcome was replied to by Mayor Mundy, Louis Blake Duff, secretary of the club and George D. Hunt, the treasurer.

His Worship was in an amiable mood, and he told many incidents of the trip to St. Louis and Chicago. He told of the banquet

the Wanderers of Chicago tendered the football party, but he said of all the towns and cities visited there was no place like Galt. Canada was God's country and Galt was the best town in it, and the football team that represented the town brought honour to it.

George D. Hunt who followed the mayor, gave a record of the expenses of the trip which totalled over $400.

Secretary Duff, the next speaker, gave an excellent address. He was both witty and serious, and he had the crowd applauding and laughing continually. He thanked the people of Galt for their reception of the team. He took exception to the statement in a Toronto paper that the team had only won a lot of tin-pot medals. The reason such a statement was made was doubtless due to the fact that a Toronto team had not won the aforesaid medals, which he knew as a matter of fact cost the St. Louis Fair people $220 – wholesale.

Gen. A. Clare, M.P., Hon. Jas. Young, Alderman Goldie, Buchanan and Cowan, J. W. Porteous, President of the Club and Chas. Cumming all gave short complimentary addresses.

Mrs. Eddie West, W. Harper and Ed. C. Codling rendered solos in a very acceptable manner.

After the reception, the team proceeded to the YMCA supper where they received additional congratulations and honour.

1906 Marathon Billy Sherring To Athens by Horse

The Marathon. The very name stirred every Greek's imagination with memories of a distant and glorious past. Every Greek youngster could recite the story by heart.

The Persians and the Athenians engaged in pitched battle on the Plains of Marathon — twenty-five miles from Athens. Outnumbered ten to one, the Athenians sent their runner, Pheidippedes, to Sparta, 150 miles away, to bring help. Pheidippedes crossed the many hills and valleys of rough terrain only to discover the Spartans were unable to help because they were in the midst of religious observances.

Pheidippides immediately began the long, lonely run back to give the Athenians his news. As he neared the encampment, the Athenian leader Miltiades met the runner. The Athenians had defeated the enemy. "Run!" he told Pheidippides. "Tell Athens of our victory!"

Running into the centre of Athens, the courier earned a place in the hearts of all Greeks forever. "Rejoice," he said, "We conquer." And with those words, Pheidippides collapsed and died.

In the original Olympic Games

there was no such race as the Marathon. The Greeks would likely have considered a race of over twenty-six miles excessive. However, with the revival of the Games in 1896, the decision to include such a race was immediately and enthusiastically accepted by the hosting Athenians. When the first winner turned out to be a Greek, a link with the glorious past had been forged. Spyridon Louis was immediately a national hero.

That was 1896. In 1900 the Games were held in Paris and a Frenchman won the Marathon; in 1904, they were held in St. Louis, and an American was the winner. In 1905 the International Olympic Committee announced a special 1906 Olympics to be held in Athens to commemorate the tenth anniversary of the revival. Although today these could be called a "Phantom Olympics", since they are not now considered to be part of the Games, the winners were given the title of "Olympic Champion" as well as the Olympic medals.

May 1, 1906. Fifty-seven competitors, twenty-six of them from Greece, prepared themselves for the start of the Marathon while their handlers sped up the race course on their bicycles to position themselves to better minister to their runners. It was hot, 27°C (80°F) in the shade. It would be a test of endurance worthy of Pheidippides.

Canadian Billy Sherring had a confident air. His home, Hamilton, was half a world away. He wondered what his fellow members of the St. Patrick's Athletic Club were

doing. A glance down at the huge green shamrock on his shirt gave him a comfortable feeling, even though it now hung loosely on his 5 foot, 6 inch frame. During his two-month stay in Greece his weight had dropped from 135 pounds to his present 112 pounds. By the end of the day, his weight would drop to 98!

It was three o'clock; the gun sounded! They were off! Sherring was in no hurry to jump into the lead. He had learned from the Boston Marathon back in 1900. There too, he was full of anticipation. He had felt fit and ready, but he wasn't prepared for the fast pace. At the 16-mile mark, with a good lead, he had collapsed and was revived too late to catch club mate Jack Caffery, the winner. He would never let it happen again.

After all, with some eleven years running experience he had faced some pretty good rivals and had come away with more than his share of wins. By 1903, he had an impressive string of victories to his credit: victories at the Barton Fair, the Hamilton Herald Road Race, a 20 mile race at Guelph, a new Canadian record for 10 miles at Milton with a time of 56:20.

Ten miles coasted by. He was a half mile behind the leaders. The time elapsed was 56 minutes – pretty close to his record pace at Milton. He thought back over the strange circumstances that brought him to Greece. When the Panhellenic Games were announced, the wheels were set in motion to send three prominent Hamilton athletes – Sherring, Caffery and Kerr – to

Athens, Greece. A proposal to raise the money by a civic fund was vetoed by City Council, so the St. Patrick's Athletic Club stepped in with plans to hold a public concert. Seventy-five dollars was raised – a lot of money, but not enough to get to Athens. Dejected and slightly cynical, Billy Sherring walked into the Commercial Hotel to talk to his friend and advisor, William "Butch" Collier. The hotel was downtown next to the City Hall; Collier, the bartender, was a popular man who always seemed to know the "inside" news. Butch certainly knew his horses, and Eddie Whyte, a trainer, had tipped Butch about "Cicely", a horse which was a "cinch" to pay at least six to one.

With nothing to lose, Sherring turned the seventy-five dollars over to Butch. The bet was made and, just as Butch said, the horse won! The money was raised and he could go to Athens!

As quickly as he could, Sherring made arrangements to leave for Athens. It didn't matter that his accommodations were third class. Or that it was a cattle boat. He was on his way to Athens for the Marathon.

He arrived in Greece near the end of February. He ran every other day so as not to tire out his body. His training, the hot sun and the strange Greek food took 23 pounds off his weight. For a time he was lonely, but his spirits were buoyed when the Canadian contingent of John Linden, Elwood Hughes and Ed Archibald arrived from Toronto on March 29. By that time, Mrs. McTaggart's boarding

house had been found and the four Canadians and four Australians moved in.

He recalled how thrilled he was when he covered the famous Marathon course in his trial run – a full fourteen minutes under the winning time of the 1896 run. He felt even better when he watched one hundred Greeks run the same course in a pre-Olympic contest. His practice time was still better than the winner's.

And now all the preparations seemed worthwhile; even coming to Marathon a day early. It was uncomfortable sleeping in the old barn on the floor with the sounds and smells of the livestock, but at least he didn't have to worry about being late to the starting line.

Sherring suddenly became conscious of hoofbeats. It was the official timer following him, now the leader, to ensure against any irregularities. He opened up a large lead but haunted by the memory of Boston, he slowed down and walked a short time. He refreshed himself with an orange and had his face bathed with water and alcohol by an Englishman in the crowd.

The roar of the cannon signalled that the leader was four kilometres from the finish. Inside the Stadium, the noise was deafening in anticipation of a Greek victory. Seventy thousand pairs of eyes strained to see, off in the distance, the insignia

Moments from his gold medal victory, Billy Sherring completes the final lap of the Marathon accompanied by Crown Prince Constantine of Greece.

of the leader. As Sherring made his way into the entrance of the huge enclosure, the cheers and cries stopped. The hushed expectancy was followed by a murmur of disappointment as Sherring's shamrock, mistaken for the Maple Leaf of Canada, came into view. Then the huge throng erupted into approving cheers as Crown Prince Constantine met Sherring at the entrance and escorted him to the finish.

It was a sight to behold: the Crown Prince, resplendently dressed, running beside a bone-tired Billy Sherring, fedora on his head, shamrock on his shirt and Union Jack in his hand – the prince and the pauper running the last half lap together. His time was 2:15 – seven minutes ahead of second-place Svamberg and four minutes ahead of the previous record.

Had he been Greek, Sherring's harvest of rewards would have included a statue of himself, a loaf of bread, free shaves, three cups of coffee a day and a weekly luncheon for six for the rest of his days – all incentives offered by Greek businessmen to the youth of the country. As it was, Sherring only wanted a hot bath, but people kept opening bottles of wine for him to drink! He was also given a young lamb, bouquets of flowers, proposals of marriage, a six-foot statue of Athene, was made an honorary citizen of Marathon, and of course, received a gold medal.

The twenty-nine-year-old Sherring was proud, but he was also homesick, and made preparations the next day for the long trip home

to Hamilton.

His victory was front page news across Canada. In Hamilton, special flags flew from the fire halls. The King wired his congratulations as did the Governor-General. On his return voyage, Sherring was given a tour of London before making his way across the Atlantic to New York, where fifty former Hamiltonians met him and feted him until his train left for Montreal.

Stating that he had done more for athletics than any other man had done for years, the Montreal Amateur Athletic Association banded together with the other athletic clubs in the city to give him a spirited reception. He was the toast of the town. An itinerary of plays, luncheons and baseball games was arranged, and it was at a luncheon in Montreal that Sherring stated his intention of retiring. After eleven years he was satisfied that he had reached the top. In a frolicking display of enthusiasm, Sherring left Montreal carried on the shoulders of his admirers to the departure gate of Windsor Station.

Toronto was the scene of another round of festivities. At a baseball game, Sherring was encouraged to treat the fans to a one-mile run. The spectators enthusiastically contributed the sum of $1269.70 which was turned over to the champion along with a gift from the city of Toronto of $400. At the departure dock, the Toronto multitudes were joined by so many Hamiltonians who made the trip across the lake to catch an early glimpse of their idol that it was necessary to enlist

the services of a second steamer to carry all the faithful admirers across the lake back to Hamilton.

When the steamer *Modjeska* made its way to the James Street dock in Hamilton, thousands of torches blazed as far as the eyes could see. A triumphal procession of carriages complete with civic dignitaries, schoolboys, bands, lodges and athletic greats such as Ned Hanlan and Lou Scholes stretched almost half the length of the parade route. It was an emotional display of enthusiasm never before seen in Hamilton. Mayor Biggar announced that the government was giving him a purse of $5000:

> . . . Your fellow citizens rejoice with you in the honours you have won by your indomitable pluck and marvellous endurance, your achievement being rendered all the more creditable by the fact that you entered the great undertaking practically alone, thereby demonstrating your confidence in your own ability to win the much coveted wreath, and also showing the world the material of which our Canadian manhood is made. . . .

Sherring retired from his competitive marathon career to become coach of the 1908 Olympic marathon team. He worked in Hamilton as a Customs Officer until his retirement in 1942. After his death on September 5, 1964, the Around the Bay Road Race, the oldest long distance road race in North America, became known as the Billy Sherring Memorial Road Race.

Alexandra Studio

1908
200m
Bobby Kerr
The Fireman

Bobby Kerr was born in Enniskillen, Ireland. In 1899, when he was seven years old his family settled in Hamilton, Ontario. For his father, George Kerr, Hamilton was the ideal city to locate himself and his young family. There were plenty of good jobs available and a sizeable Irish community, called Corktown, among the population of forty-two thousand people.

Two other prominent athletic members of the Irish community, Jack Caffery and Bill Sherring turned to long distance running, and were largely responsible for the "Marathon craze" which struck Hamilton at the turn of the century. But long distance running wasn't for Bobby Kerr. He noticed that in school games and impromptu races he was faster than others. It was that speed which helped him land his job with the International Harvester Fire Brigade at the turn of the century. Factories made a big thing of the speed of their firemen, and in competitions against other firms or demonstrations of techniques, Kerr's speed was a great asset.

It was as a twenty-year-old in 1902 that Kerr gave an indication of what the future might hold. The Coronation Games at Victoria Park were part of a program to celebrate the accession of Edward VII in the new era of the horseless carriage and the age of speed. It was at those games that Kerr won the 100, 440 and 800 yard events and made such an impression that he earned civic recognition for his athletic ability.

Kerr seemed to find his niche in

the shorter distance events. His jack rabbit start at a time when there were no starting blocks made him an ideal sprinter and on one occasion actually saved his life. In 1907, he went to the train station to meet the Toronto baseball club on its way through to Columbus, Ohio. While he was busy speaking to the players in the coach, the train began to pull out of the station. Kerr jumped off. There were two sets of tracks between the car and the platform; a stationary car was on the track closer to him. Kerr walked around it and headed onto the next track. A yard engine came thundering down toward him. His sprinter's start saved his life by inches.

He was ranked as a "scratch runner" at a time when handicapping was fashionable. Opponents were always given a head start while Kerr ran from the starting line – usually nothing more than a scratch across the cinder track. This arrangement always insured that Kerr was running behind someone, a fact that contributed to the great acceleration he had developed.

For four years, victory and Bobby Kerr seemed inseparable. Track and field had greater prominence in those days and many meets which no longer run today – the Hamilton Labour Day Games, Canadian YMCA Championships, Montreal Caledonian Games, Toronto Irish-Canadian Games, the Amateur Athletic Union of Canada Games – provided a proving ground for the budding olympian. In the year 1907 alone, Kerr was first in over forty events.

The Olympic Games were Kerr's real ambition. The disappointment was almost too great to bear when enough money couldn't be raised to send the twenty-four-year-old to the 1906 Olympics. When his fellow Hamiltonian Billy Sherring won the Marathon at those Games, Kerr was even more determined to represent Canada in 1908.

Elaborate trials were to be held in different sections of the country in an effort to choose the best team available for the London Games. With Kerr's wins in the 100 and 200 m events at the Ontario and Dominion trials, his dream was close to being fulfilled. Kerr would represent Hamilton and Canada at the 1908 Games in London.

The Stadium in London was impressive: iron grandstands surrounded the huge track. There were an impressive 63 000 seats, a capacity of more than 100 000 with standing room. Within the 660 m cycle track was a 536.45 m cinder running track, and within this, a full-sized soccer field and a 100 m swimming pool. Everything seemed to be there, platforms for wrestling, gymnastics and a hall for fencers. It was quite a change for Kerr. At St. Louis, the Games were held to publicize the Fair, but at London there was no doubt about it, the Games were the focus. He was determined to use the two weeks remaining to prepare himself for the 100 and 200 m events.

On July 4, the British Championships were held at Shepherd's Bush. Not only would these events serve as a trial competition for judges and officials, they would also be valuable practice for the athletes. It was a satisfying day for Bobby Kerr. He not only won the 100 and 220 yard events with the appropriate gold medals and cups for each, he was also awarded the Gold Cup as the most outstanding performer of the games. All this made him feel confident. But even more so, he was pleased because he had defeated Walker, the young South African some were touting as the favourite of the Games, and Morton, the four-time English champion who had handed Kerr one of his rare defeats in the 100 yard event of the Montreal Caledonian Games of 1905.

There was a great deal of newspaper coverage about the Olympic Games, but a combination of daily rain and high prices served to attract only small crowds. Within a week of the opening, prices were lowered in an attempt to attract more spectators. By coincidence it was also time for the beginning of the heats for the 100 and 200 m events.

On July 14, Kerr won his heat in the 100. The next day he won again, as well as his first of the 200 m trials. On a track heavy from the continuous rain, Kerr's best time for the 100 m during the trials was 11 s. Both Walker of South Africa and Rector of the United States equalled the Olympic record of 10.8 s.

On Wednesday, July 16, at 1:00 p.m., Kerr ran in the 200 m semifinal winning it in 22.4 s. It was also the day of the 100 m final and Kerr's first attempt at the elusive gold. Kerr, anxious to regain some of his strength, was rubbed down and took a taxi to his quarters for a rest in bed before his return for the 100 m finals at 4:00 p.m.

There was no gold in the 100 m race for Bobby Kerr. The nineteen-year-old South African, Walker, whom Kerr had beaten earlier, shot past Kerr and Rector at the 55 m mark and went on to win the event in 10.8 s. Kerr and the American Rector, finished in a dead heat and it was only after much deliberation that Rector was awarded second place and Kerr third. Disappointment enveloped Kerr. Twenty-four hours later, however, he would have a second chance for a gold. It would be his sixth race in three days, all against world-class competition. He became even more introspective in preparation for his second "Battle at Shepherd's Bush".

His plan was simple: he had to get off to a good start and be in a commanding position after 140 m. His opposition weren't sprinters in the 100 m sense. He knew that if he could get out in front while still accelerating, he could do it, he could win the gold. At the start, Kerr's unorthodox stance set him apart. Others crouched in their stance with thumb and fingers spread parallel to the finish line; Kerr's four fingers on each hand pointed toward the finish line, his thumb away. With the crack of the starter's gun, Kerr was off, his body leaning forward as if being pulled by a powerful string. His stride lengthened. He had the appearance of a sleek greyhound drawing away from the pack. At 140 m, Kerr was well in the lead, his momentum built up to the point where acceleration was no longer

Bobby Kerr as the Manager of the Canadian Olympic track and field team in 1932. It was the last time Canada won a gold medal in track and field.

possible. The gold medal was his! He breasted the tape in the time of 22.6 s over the slow track. Immediately, he was overwhelmed by his teammates who hoisted him to their shoulders. Amid wild enthusiasm they erupted into their cheer:

Hya-yaka! Hya-yaka!
Canada! Canada!
Boom-a-laka! Boom-a-laka!
Cis, Boom-Boom-er-ah!
Across the sea –
C-A-N-A-D-A
Hurrah!

Thousands of miles away in Hamilton, word of Kerr's victory was received with jubilation. Spe-cial flags were put out. The huge bell in the James Street city hall started pealing its good news and immediately was joined by hundreds of bells and whistles throughout the city. Even while congratulatory telegrams were being sent to Kerr from the Mayor, the Tiger Football Club, the Rowing Club, International Harvester and a host of other organizations, preparations were made to welcome home the new champion.

In 1912, Kerr had an opportunity to represent his city and country once more in the Olympic Games. Even after having earned his position, he deferred and stepped aside to offer his place to a younger athlete who would benefit from the experience.

His active running career was to flare again briefly during the First War. After joining the 205th Battalion, he transferred to the 5th division's 164th Battalion and engaged in several competitions overseas. As a captain of the 1928 Canadian Olympic team, he oversaw the best performances ever turned in by a Canadian team in Olympic competition. In 1932, as manager of the track and field division, he was there for Canada's last gold medal in track and field.

Bobby Kerr was elected to Canada's Sports Hall of Fame in 1955 and passed away in May, 1963. Upon his death, memories, reminiscences and the identification of the man with his city were all resurrected. Another era was revived only to lapse back into the past and the distant haze of memories long forgotten.

1908
Lacrosse
The All Canadas
The Fun
Is in
Getting There

There's so much more fun to be had in entering a competition that you're sure of winning! After all, hadn't lacrosse been invented in Canada? Did anybody really think that South Africa could field a team that was going to be any kind of a contest for our best? Could Australia be serious? Didn't our Canadian Lacrosse Association team, the All Canadas they were called, beat them easily during their tour of the Antipodes in '07? And the All Canadas had been beaten by every Canadian team before it left for Down Under! That lacrosse team even beat the Aussies at hockey on their funny indoor artificial ice. England might be tougher, but the Ottawa Capitals had no problems on their tour of the UK. Surely the national team chosen for the 1908 Olympics was the strongest aggregation ever assembled – a cinch for the gold.

That was the prevailing feeling as the Canadians prepared to defend the gold medal won by the Winnipeg Shamrocks in 1904. The fun was going to be in the journey, not the destination. How often do the colonials get the chance to go over 'ome and show them how to do it?

Twenty thousand dollars had been raised to send teams in track and field, trapshooting, rowing, tennis and golf. There wasn't enough money for soccer, rugby, hockey or skating, but there was enough for a lacrosse team. Choosing the players set off a controversy that threatened not only lacrosse, but hockey as well.

Lacrosse and hockey were sea-sonal in those days before artificial ice was widespread and many athletes played in both sports for year-round training. When Trustee William Foran ruled that the Stanley Cup was to be presented to the best team in Canada whether or not its players were paid, there was a rush by every team to attract good players by paying them. The Amateur Athletic Union of Canada stepped in and declared that every-one who was paid or played with or against someone who was paid, was a professional. Frenzied lacrosse players then formed the rival Athletic Federation of Canada which promptly declared that ama-teurs would remain amateurs as long as they did not personally receive any money.

By coincidence, the same William Foran, an active member of the Athletic Federation, was selected by the Central Olympic Committee to choose the Canadian lacrosse representatives to the 1908 London Olympics. This team was to have national representation as there wasn't any single team made up entirely of amateurs that was strong enough.

So a concept dictated by circum-stances became a great publicity-filled venture. Reports from London told about British efforts to choose an all-star team which would pro-vide tough competition for the Canadians. The Canadians would have to be a "top flight aggrega-tion in order to be successful", warned Emmanuel Tasse, president of the Ottawa Capitals. The rival associations declared their inten-tion to cooperate to the fullest.

Individual teams indicated their willingness to incorporate exhibi-tion games against the Olympic team into their schedules; players' services were offered. Nothing ap-peared to be too good for the novice national team. After years of wrangling, the cooperation in la-crosse circles was like a breath of fresh air. Lacrosse teams in To-ronto, Montreal, Ottawa, Cornwall and Quebec City vied with each other in the interest of this new crusade. It seemed too good to be true.

It was. Among the thirty-five candidates whose amateur stand-ing was above reproach, President Kerns of the Canadian Lacrosse Association voiced the hope that his organization would be propor-tionately represented among the fifteen to be chosen. There was pressure that the West and French Canada would be suitably recog-nized. Exhibition games with the Toronto teams were juggled and scheduled to avoid games within the league. Ottawa refused to honour its commitment to play the nationals; club officials were upset that Tommy Gorman, a standout with Ottawa, played with the Olympians rather than with the Capitals against the Montreal Shamrocks in a league contest. The agreement between the two rival amateur bodies threatened to erupt into the open again.

News travelled from London that the AFC representative, William Boyd, supported the American motion to declare Canadian Tom Longboat a professional and there-fore make him ineligible for the

Henry Hoobin, one of four players from the Montreal Shamrocks who joined the All Canadas. Interestingly, the Montreal players were the only ones not afflicted by seasickness during the team's ocean crossing.

George Rennie and Alex "Dad" Turnbull from New Westminster's Minto Cup Champions. Turnbull was said to be the best Canadian lacrosse player of his day.

Marathon. Foran was clearly upset and, much to the joy of the AAUC, resigned from the Federation. Meanwhile, the news was also received that South Africa and Australia would not be represented. Only Canada and England would field teams.

And so on October 2, 1908, a jubilant throng congregated at Windsor Station in Montreal for the train ride to Quebec City to board the *Empress of Britain.* Fifteen Canadian lacrosse players were the object of hundreds of well wishers. Seven were from the Montreal area: Brennan, Hoobin, Dillon and Fyon from the Shamrocks, McKerrow and Hamilton from the Amateur Athletic Association team, and Duckett from the Nationals. New Westminster's Minto Cup champions sent two: Rennie and Turnbull, a forty-four-year-old de-

The All Canadas Lacrosse Team appearing a bit apprehensive just before their Olympic match with the British. A few hours later their moods changed drastically as they became Olympic gold medallists.

scribed as the best lacrosse player in Canada. Calgary sent McLeod; Ottawa, Gorman; Cornwall, Broderick. Mara came from Toronto, Dixon from St. Catharines and Campbell from Orangeville.

A holiday atmosphere prevailed at the station. Over a continuous din, subdued only by great blasts of steam from the Empress Express, well-wishers shouted words of encouragement. As the train huffed and puffed out of the station, the silence between blasts of smoke was punctuated with loud cheers from the crowd, spurred on by Fyon, Brennan, Murphy and Lally waving farewell from the rear platform.

The voyage from Quebec City to Liverpool was made in good time – eight days – but for most of the party it was an eternity. Gales and high winds buffeted the boat continuously. All the players were seasick – all, that is, except Hoobin, Brennan, Fyon and Murphy who happily roamed about the ship in good spirits, even venturing ''below'' to the engine room, where the fine points of the machinery and details about the boilers of the oceangoing vessel were explained by the chief engineer.

For the others, Liverpool and terra firma came none too soon. The eight-day trip had been a numbing experience. Even the train ride from Liverpool to London was looked upon with mixed emotions, but at least the swaying of the train wasn't as bad as the gyrations of the ship. For the Irish group, however, Liverpool was but a launching point for the highlight

of the trip – a quick visit to Ireland.

It was a joyous time which passed all too quickly; then they were off to London to meet up with the rest of the team and play the match against England for the gold medal and the Olympic Championship.

The Canadian team, wearing white sweaters and green piping with a green maple leaf in the centre (in honour of the large number of Irish on the team), won the match with a 14–10 score. The English played with an abundance of enthusiasm but not enough finesse. Trailing 6–2 at the half, the British tied the score at 9–9 at the end of the third quarter, but the Canadians outscored them 5 to 1 in the last quarter.

Aside from the gold medal, the game was a fine display of sportsmanship. When Dillon broke his stick during play and was having difficulty finding a replacement, an English player, Martin, offered to stay out until Dillon returned. At the end of the contest, players exchanged sticks, shook hands and congratulated each other on a game well played. A steady stream of visitors came to the Canadians' dressing room including the Lord

Mayor of London and the Olympics' organizers, Earl Roberts and Lord Desborough.

Excitement and cheers greeted the announcement that the team had been invited to play games at Manchester and Stockport. The hospitality of the English and the camaraderie of the Canadians were such that there wasn't any great hurry to return home. Each city was the site of another lacrosse and social victory for the tourists. Again the Irish contingent was in the middle of the festivities. At a banquet at Stockport, the evening program was drawn up to include a song by Paddy Brennan. His face alternated between shades of white and green as the Master of Ceremonies announced that ''Captain Brennan, who has the reputation of being one of the sweetest singers in Canada, will sing the Maple Leaf''. While a sputtering Brennan sat amid the applause wondering whether he should inflict his torturous voice on the gathering, Gus Dillon, smiling at the joke played on Brennan, arose and ''being the possessor of a fine voice'' sang for him.

On November 4, 1908, the *Empress of Ireland* returned to Quebec on a record-breaking Atlantic crossing. A large crowd was on hand to meet its champion passengers, the All Canada Lacrosse Team of 1908. All received a loud cheer and long ovation – all that is except Hoobin, Dillon and Brennan who weren't on the boat at all. They had decided to return to Ireland to look up old friends and relations!

Alexandra Studio

1912 Trapshooting Walter Ewing The Forgotten Canadian

Walter Ewing is not the best known of Canadians. Some sources list him as a winner in the trapshooting events of the 1900 Games, but since the event was staged for the first time in 1908, they are certainly in error. In fact, Walter Ewing did not even start his trapshooting career until 1905. How-ever it is no error that Ewing did win a gold medal in trapshooting at the 1908 Games in London.

While the Games were to include a variety of sports, by far the most publicity in Canada was being generated by the track and field events, particularly the Marathon. Copious newspaper accounts described the various trials which were taking place throughout the country while trapshooting was relegated to a minimum of informa-tion, if indeed it was mentioned at all.

Vying for space with track and field in general was the unfolding saga of the Canadian runner, Tom Longboat, and his irrepressible manager, Tom Flanagan. Long-boat, a winner of almost every long distance event he entered, was considered to be a sure winner of the Marathon. Flanagan took the "bronzed warrior" to Ireland to train for the Games and sent back daily reports to inform the readers in Canada of every move made by his protégé. But the medal which was a certainty did not materialize. In the Marathon, which itself was heavily publicized because of ir-regularities, Longboat collapsed after eighteen miles.

"Walter Ewing is not the best known of Canadians." The pic-ture here appears to be the only existing photographic record of this forgotten Canadian gold medallist.

All of these events had the effect of pushing trapshooting and Walter Ewing further into the background. Even though shooting had a long history in Canada, it was rifle shooting and the Bisley competitions which were occasions for celebrations. Rifle shooting had more of a mass interest than trapshooting which, because it was derived from the traditionally aristocratic sport of the hunt, had a narrower appeal.

Because of this, few people would have noted that on the grounds of the Montreal Gun Club in mid April, 1908, the trapshooting champion of Quebec, R. B. Hutchinson, defeated Walter Ewing 84 birds to 80 in the 100 shots allowed, thereby retaining his championship.

Ewing and Hutchinson met again later in April at the St. Hubert Gun Club in Ottawa with reversed results. It was the second successive victory for Ewing since his defeat; he had previously won the Montreal Gun Club's Good Friday Shoot.

There was good reason for the flurry of shooting competitions. With the Olympic Games approaching and the decision to send as complete a Canadian Team as possible, Olympic trials were necessary. Marksmen needed all the pressure of competition they could get before the trapshooting trials at Toronto in May.

Curiously enough, fifteen were chosen after those Toronto heats, of which six would form the final team. There was always the possibility that one might not be able to get time off work or otherwise be unable to go. It appears that the

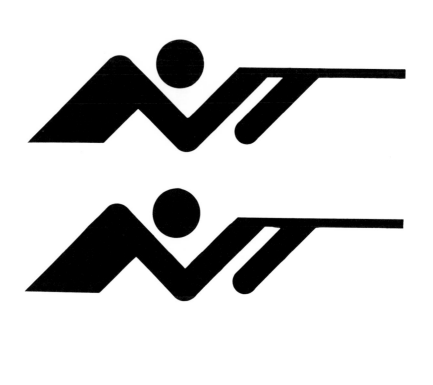

46

selection of the team might have been based on ability to shoot coupled with availability of time and/or money to help defray expenses.

Thus among the hopeful ninety-one athletes of Canada's first representative team at the Olympics, the first trapshooting competitors boarded the *Tunisian* for the long trip to London. Ewing and the other five seemed to be apart from the rest. Publicity was reserved for the track people and officials; the trapshooting team continued to exist in a cloak of anonymity which had been tailored for them back in Canada.

Perhaps Ewing might have thought that this would change when the team arrived in London. Yet once the Games started, events forced Ewing and his shooting mates even further into the background.

Massive amounts of publicity resulted from a variety of incidents that infuriated competing nations. Swedish and American flags were not among those surrounding the stadium stands. Finland, ordered by the Russians to fly the Russian flag, refused and marched in the opening ceremonies without one. The flag debate continued when the United States' athletes refused to dip the Stars and Stripes to the British King, immediately setting off another uproar. The Irish were furious because they marched and competed under the colours of Great Britain rather than Ireland.

On top of these competitive diversions the trapshooting team had even more to contend with. As if to reinforce its detachment from the mainstream of Olympic life, the trapshooting competition was to be held at far-off Uxendon and under British rules.

In Canada the sport was rather predictable. Clay birds were thrown from one central point; they might fly at several different angles but because they started from the one source, it was possible to keep the gun trained on the delivery point and follow the bird on its flight. In England, the traps were installed below ground level in a twenty-seven-foot trench. When the signal was given, the clay bird might go off from any point along the trench – and in any direction.

It was a difficult adjustment for Ewing and the rest of the Canadian team. He had been used to aiming the gun at the launching point. With conditions at Uxendon being different, a whole new approach to shooting was required.

Every spare moment he had he studied the English style. He conditioned himself to hold the gun at his chest, both eyes open and ready to sight the bird. Reaction became extremely important. The gun had to be moved from the chest to the shoulder once the bird was launched. Quick aim had to be taken, the shot made and the gun returned to its waiting position. To make matters worse, the birds occasionally blended into a background of trees making their sighting even more difficult.

Not one of the sixty-one competitors really expected the Canadians to perform well. In a shorter competition they might be able to hit a hot streak but the Olympic event seemed to be set up to avoid that sort of possibility. Eighty birds were to be launched in three different stages. In the first, thirty were set off in two different sets of fifteen each. Ewing recorded a score of 27. Twenty more birds were fired; Ewing hit eighteen. Thirty more birds were to be launched and to add to the suspense each of the sixty-one competitors were to shoot at ten each on three separate occasions.

Ewing, showing amazing consistency, was on target 27 times. His final score, 72 of 80, was far ahead of his closest rival, teammate George Beattie of Hamilton who scored 60. In spite of the odds, Ewing had won a gold medal and Beattie a silver. In addition, the remarkable duo had led their teammates to a near upset, losing the team event by a slim margin of two birds, 423–421.

Walter Ewing's victory, unlike Bobby Kerr's, brought no riotous celebrations. When his competition finished, he booked passage on the *Empress of Britain* and left for home. Rather than waiting until the closing ceremonies to receive his medals, he asked his teammates to collect them from Queen Alexandra.

In 1912, Ewing was again asked to represent Canada in the Stockholm Olympics, but had to decline because of the pressures of his family's coal business. Today, Walter Ewing continues to be overshadowed, just as he appeared to be on that cloudy English day in 1908 when he won a gold medal for Canada.

1912 10 000m George Goulding The Heel-and-Toe Star

The year was 1903. A slim, dark teenager from Hull, England, stood looking at a stretch of bleak Alberta prairie. The wind blew forlornly and the young man wished fervently that he was home. But going home wasn't possible. His father was dead and there was no money for a return passage. George Goulding turned his back on the prairie and made his way to Toronto and international fame.

Goulding's beginnings as a celebrity were innocuous enough. As a young boy he was a good swimmer, gymnast and runner. When he first joined the Toronto Central YMCA as a teenager fresh from his shocking exposure to Alberta, he joined as a marathon runner. Marathon running had become very popular in Canada due to the exploits of such famous runners as Tom Longboat. Goulding was at best a fair distance runner,

winning only occasionally, but never quitting a race. On a whim one day he turned to heel-and-toe racing.

After pacing a friend in a practice walk, Goulding was persuaded to enter a local race. Thanks to his marvellous coordination and his great endurance, he was easily the winner and was congratulated for his efficient style. In his entire career he was never once warned by the judges for unfair walking — though it was not unusual for even the world's best walkers to be disqualified several times each year for "lifting". This infraction was based on the rule that one foot had to be in contact with the ground at all times. When both feet were off the ground it was considered run-

ning, which, of course, was disallowed. Goulding's style was beyond reproach even in his famous "sprints". It helped make him the best in the world for several years.

After his initial triumph, George entered about a half-dozen races in the spring of 1908 and finally the Canadian Championships. In this meet, after less than three months at the sport, Goulding defeated the reigning champion, Charles Skene, to gain a place on the Canadian Olympic team.

The Canadians selected were to compete in what was only the fourth Olympiad, (not counting the extra Olympiad held in the "off" year of 1906), and the organization of the Olympics up until then had been very loose. The 1908 London Olympics changed all that. These Games saw, for example, the first attempt at standardizing the rules of competition, and the first Olym-

pic report on a Canadian team, written by their manager, J. H. Crocker. The 1908 Olympics were a milestone in both the history of the Games and the career of George Goulding.

The young Goulding threw his slight 5 foot, 10 inch, 142-pound frame into training with his usual zest and determination. No one gave him much chance at winning an Olympic medal, but he got full marks for dedication to the task. Entered in the 3500 m walk after being in the sport only two and one-half months did not faze the young Canadian. In England he won his heat and entered the final against the formidable Larner of England.

Larner was a veteran and world champion at age thirty-eight. Also in the final was E. J. Webb of England, another veteran walker. Their experience made all the difference, as Larner won with Webb second. Goulding finished fourth, but his walking style was remarked on by the judges. Goulding also learned a lot that was to help him later. He noted, for example, that the champion, Larner, used a special shoe that was extremely light and had a very thin rubber sole. In the years to come, Goulding was to put the lessons learned in the 1908 Olympics to good use.

Having finished with the event he was sent to enter, Goulding looked around the London Olympics for something to do. He entered the 10 000 m walk and finished last. He was not perturbed by this. He figured it was the beginning of his training for the 1912 Olympics. To

complete his stay in London, he also entered the Marathon race even though there were already eleven other Canadians entered. Eight of the Canadian marathoners finished in the top twenty-five, and tireless, versatile Goulding was among them. He completed the distance in 3:33:26 to place twenty-second.

The taste of Olympic competition stayed with George Goulding. He plunged into training after he returned home. He raced in a three-mile handicap race in Hamilton and won it. He also won a ten-mile walk in Guelph. Winter was no reason to break training for Goulding. He sometimes trained by snow-shoeing, and there were many indoor races. By the end of the year he owned all but one Canadian record at every distance up to ten miles. The record looked like this:

1 mile	6:45	Skene
2 mile	13:01	Goulding
3 mile	28:25	Goulding
4 mile	31:39	Goulding
5 mile	39:45	Goulding
6 mile	48:06	Goulding
7 mile	56:27	Goulding
8 mile	1:05:02.6	Goulding
9 mile	1:13:23.6	Goulding
10 mile	1:21:42.4	Goulding

By the year 1910 his fame as a walker had begun to spread. Invitations to compete in the US came and Goulding began what was to

Webb of England shows the strain of trying to keep up with the tireless Goulding in a match race held at Toronto's CNE Stadium in the summer of 1910.

be a long and popular love affair with the US sporting public. In January of that year he beat the US champion Leibgold in the two-mile distance. He not only beat him, but lapped him and broke the US record which had stood for 25 years, by a remarkable 14 s!

It was decided that Goulding should race against E. Webb of England in a match race in Toronto. The arrangements were duly made and with much fanfare and newspaper coverage Webb came to Canada to train and acclimatize himself in the summer of 1910. (He was later to stay and live for a few years in Manitoba.) The mile race was held before a crowd of 15 000 in Toronto's CNE Stadium. Goulding won easily. Webb commented after the race that his better distance was three miles. His challenge was accepted and later that afternoon Goulding sprinted away from him, delighting the crowd and winning handily.

The demand for Goulding's services at track meets rose with his increasing prowess. He was asked to appear in New York, Buffalo and Toronto. He was forced to become selective. Attending too many meets was as bad as competing in too few. He raced in a major competition about twice per month all year long. Newspaper accounts of his walking style compared him favourably to the Olympic champion, Larner. The English papers, without having seen Goulding, accused him of walking illegally. The mail to newspaper editors was heavy enough that the T. Eaton Company, through their employees' athletic

association, arranged to bring Larner to Canada for another match race in 1911.

George Larner had been dethroned as the world record holder in the mile but still held all the remaining outdoor records up to ten miles. Thus, the race arranged for the Island Stadium was billed almost as a grudge match. Before another capacity crowd, Goulding beat Larner by over 30 yards in 6:32, and the stands erupted while George's Central YMCA teammates hoisted him to their shoulders and paraded him triumphantly before the crowd.

In a three-mile race about one week later at Scarborough, Goulding got off to a very fast start over Larner. Larner, having trouble, was making a valiant effort to catch up and the judges fell to the track to scrutinize his pace very carefully. Larner had a reputation for "lifting" and he had been disqualified in England twice that same year. This, plus the fact that a sharp newspaper photographer had caught a picture of Larner in training with both feet off the ground, gave the judges extra reason to suspect him. Thus with Goulding rapidly pulling away, and judges down flat on the track examining his feet, Larner stopped, angry and frustrated.

Goulding, by now some hundred yards in the lead, turned to see his opponent standing still. Instead of increasing his lead with this advantage, the remarkable Goulding turned and came back. He persuaded Larner to continue with both walkers even at that spot.

Once again Goulding pulled away. He won the race and extra praise from the crowd for his sportsmanship. His time broke his own Canadian record despite the delay in the race.

The 1912 Olympic contest was almost anticlimactic for the great Goulding. The Games were held in Stockholm and there were nearly 3000 athletes in attendance. Not much chance was given for the Canadian team to win medals with the exception of Goulding whose press clippings alone would have been enough to vanquish half his competition.

On the sixth day of this very proper Olympics (the US athletes had been warned to cheer only for US and Swedish competitors) Goulding won his gold. He began two days earlier by winning his heat in the 10 000 m. In the final, Goulding jumped to a quick lead and was immediately challenged by his old rival from England, Webb. Also in the race was St. Norman of South Africa, Dumbill and Yates of England, Altimani of Italy and Rasmussen of Denmark. The race appeared routine until some very unusual actions on the part of the officials.

One official poured cold water over the head of Altimani. Another, perhaps to even things, offered Yates a glass of water which he refused. Then the officials, who were inexperienced, stooped to their business of examining the

Percy MacDonald, a race official and George Goulding before a local race in 1910.

Authors' Collection

contestants. They quickly disqualified Dumbill, St. Norman and Yates, the latter when he had only two laps left in the race. These decisions were made without consultation and were completely arbitrary and binding. Not wishing to suffer a similar fate, Goulding proceeded very carefully and still won by 80 yards over Webb in 46:28.4. His first act was to send a telegram to his wife. It was typically terse, but told the whole story. It read: "Won – George".

World War I interrupted the Olympics proposed for Berlin, and Goulding's chances for again displaying his talents on the world stage. He joined a special regiment composed of Toronto sportsmen and while training raced his last major contest. In an indoor two-mile event, he set a new world indoor record with a time of 13:37; lapping the American champion, Renz, in the process.

So the long and outstanding career of George Goulding came to a close. Years later, he was to note wryly that the plot of prairie ground he abandoned for international stardom had sprouted a couple of oil wells. He had ended up trading black gold for the real thing, and it was the sporting world and Canada that had become the richer.

George Goulding and club mate Percy MacDonald training at the Toronto North Central YMCA in 1909. Goulding originally joined the Y as a marathon runner and started heel-and-toe racing on a whim.

1912 Swimming George Hodgson
Canada's First Double Gold

George Hodgson is the only Canadian to have won a gold medal in swimming at the Olympic Games. But even more remarkable is that the eighteen-year-old won not one, but two golds. The events were the 400 and 1500 m free style; the Olympics were the 1912 Games of Stockholm, Sweden.

The Hodgson family had been part of the commercial and social centre of Montreal for many years and was famously represented in the foremost athletic club in Montreal, the Amateur Athletic Association. Lacrosse, football, hockey, curling and golf were only some of the sports in which the Hodgson boys excelled.

With George Hodgson, it was swimming. Having spent summers in the Laurentian Mountains of Quebec, much of his time was spent in or around water. Hodgson attended the High School of Montreal and was a frequent visitor to the Montreal AAA clubhouse which had one of the few indoor pools in Canada. It was there he came under the guidance of Jimmy Rose, the club's swimming instructor.

As a sixteen-year-old, Hodgson regularly defeated most of the seniors at the MAAA pool in weekly handicap races. Barely out of the junior ranks he entered the Canadian Championship in 1910, winning every race he entered.

It was becoming evident that his style was more suited to longer distances; he won a quarter-mile race in Toronto in 1910, more than a full minute ahead of his nearest rival. In 1911, when it was announced that Festival of the Empire Games would be held in London, England, it was natural that the MAAA would want to be actively represented and equally natural that George Hodgson should be selected to represent the club.

It was his first international success. He won the one mile event in the time of 25:27.6. He was a hero when he returned to Montreal, and in a grateful response, his club mates presented young Hodgson with a locket commemorating his victory. The youngster had defeated two of Britain's best known swimmers, a fact appreciated by his club as preparations were being

made for the 1912 Stockholm Games.

Hodgson entered McGill University prior to his eighteenth birthday in the fall of 1911. He had another year of successes, winning all of his events at the Canadian Championships in early 1912 and helping McGill win the Inter-collegiate swimming championships. His only losses occurred in a meet in New York where he was defeated in two separate 100 yard races.

It was during this period that Hodgson worked hardest with Rose to prepare for the Stockholm Games. They worked as brothers; Hodgson putting his heart and soul into his training. He became less satisfied with beating competitors or making good times; he was out to improve himself. The young swimmer proved easy to coach, always willing to try any experiments to better his time, always appreciative of suggestions which could help him improve. He was a model athlete to train, working hard to perfect his new style.

Every night for almost six months Hodgson followed his ritual, appearing at the MAAA and going through his paces under the guiding eye of Jimmy Rose. He had developed a fluid motion where there was very little lag, seemingly pulled along by a powerful string. His new style, developed to make all his muscles contribute rather than overtax a few, minimized the cramped feeling a swimmer might have using the Australian crawl for any distance. Even so, every night at the end of his strenuous workout he was ready for Jimmy Rose's rubdown. Hodgson was so taken with the combination

Courtesy G. K. Armstrong, McGill University

of alcohol, witch hazel and oil of wintergreen especially concocted for him that he was afraid the supply would run out leaving him without any for the Games.

An interesting parade left the pool at the headquarters of the MAAA on June 14. Two pipers and an automobile led the procession of the athletes to the ship, S.S. *Teutonic*. Each man was cheered as he walked up the gangway. McGill students as well as MAAA members were there cheering Hodgson on. For the first time the Games were not connected in any way with an exhibition and there was much publicity being generated.

The Swedes had built an adequate and practical swimming facility for the 1912 Games. A body of water at the foot of Laboratory Hill served as the swimming area. The sides were pontooned and starting and finishing areas were constructed at the ends of the 100 m pool. The bottom had been scraped; the mud removed and replaced with sand to keep the water clean.

Hodgson's first event was the 1500 m freestyle. He wasted little time in making his presence felt. In the third heat he set a world's record of 22:23. His entry into the finals was just three seconds slower, but still fast enough to win the semi-final heat.

The 1500 m final was an impressive performance by the youngster with the white cap. At the first turn he was 10 m in front, after 500 m he had a lead of 25 m. The 1000 m was covered in the world's record time of 14:37; the 1500 in 22 min for another world's record as well. He continued swimming to challenge the mile mark. His time of 23:45.5 was a world's record for that distance as well. In one race, Hodgson had set three records and won a gold medal. Commendable feats all, but they seemingly made no impression on the modest eighteen-year-old. A teammate was to recall later that "he never opened his mouth after the 1500 m swim. After he had won it he came to the house where we had our rooms and went out with the crowd for a turn around town, but the great victory was never mentioned."

In the sixth heat of the 400 m freestyle, Hodgson won easily again in 5:50.6. Swimming in the semi-final, he set a new world record and advanced to the 400 m finals. Hardwich of Australia and Hodgson were moving almost in unison during the early stages of the race

George Hodgson in 1916. Hodgson had hoped to again compete in the Olympics but the 1916 Berlin Olympics were cancelled by World War I.

for the gold, Hodgson slightly ahead. At the halfway mark both turned simultaneously, but the eighteen-year-old's hard training paid off. He edged ahead during the third lap; Hardwich fell behind and was taken over by the Britisher Hatfield. Hosgson finished 1.4 s ahead of Hatfield to win in the world record time of 5:24.4. His sixth world's record; his second gold medal.

Preparations were made to welcome Hodgson home on August 10, but he had other plans. En route to Montreal, he detoured by way of Hamburg, Germany, where he entered and won the 1500 m and

500 m races for Hamburg and Kaiser Corps. From Hamburg he travelled to Manchester where he won another 1500 m race and the Hyde Seal Cup. The whole trip was quite an accomplishment for Hodgson. He had won five cups, two Olympic gold medals, two more gold medals presented to him in Germany at Hamburg, and set six world records.

On August 19, several hundred members of the MAAA and guests gathered to pay their homage to their world champion. President Bowie of the MAAA presented Hodgson with a gold watch while the audience broke out with "For He's a Jolly Good Fellow". Alderman Emard made the City's presentation of a gold locket studded with diamonds. Hodgson seemed embarrassed by all the fuss being made. Not until he went for a swim in the pool later that evening did he seem relaxed for the first time.

Hodgson continued to win medals but of a different type. With the outbreak of the Great War, he went to England where he joined the Royal Air Force and won the AFC and the London Board of Trade Silver Medal for rescues made at sea. On his return to Canada, he continued his swimming career once again representing Canada at the 1920 Antwerp Games. There were no medals there. His 1912 records lasted until 1924 when they were eclipsed by Johnny Weissmuller of later "Tarzan" fame. His two gold medals remain even to this day, the only two golds ever won by a Canadian in Olympic swimming competition.

BETWEEN THE WARS 1920·1936

As the world experienced changes between World War I and World War II, so did the Olympic Games. Among them were the increase of events for women, especially in track and field, the gathering momentum of interest in the Games throughout the world and the addition of more pomp and ceremony such as the five-ring Olympic symbol – a mysterious design originally found on an altar on the site of the ancient Greek Olympics, and the Olympic flame and torch – again a ritual from the past, except the early Greeks used to start the fire in the chest of a human sacrifice! These changes reflected sociological and political upheavals everywhere, with the era ending as it had begun, in war.

The Olympiad of 1920 was hastily brought on the scene to maintain the four-year schedule of the event begun in 1896. The interruption of the scheduled 1916 Games, originally slated for Germany, had halted the growth of the Olympics in both world-wide interest, and in training techniques of the athletes. Quick revival after the war was imperative. Despite the fact the VI Olympiad in Antwerp staggered visibly, the holding of these Games in 1920 helped usher in the "roaring twenties" that gave the Olympics great momentum.

The dominance of the United States in the 1920–1936 span was unchallenged until the so-called "Nazi Olympics" in Berlin which closed the era. Although de Coubertin's original idea had not included the thought of scoring the Games as nation against nation, the practice slowly crept in during this time, perhaps as a natural aftermath to the war. The Nazi party turned the Games into a political stage and by winning the unofficial championship of the 1936 Olympics "proved" the superiority of totalitarianism over democracy.

In Antwerp, in 1920, the Americans were often booed for winning. Perhaps because they won so consistently; perhaps because the Europeans owed them so much for their help in World War I. Whatever the reasons, the political tides that ebbed and flowed started the between-wars Games with democracy as the leading political and athletic power and ended with fascism.

It was the "roaring twenties", however, which saw the Olympic Games bloom in keeping with the excitement of the times. As prosperity increased and memories of the war faded, cultural changes followed one after another. Perhaps one of the most significant was the rise in the status of women. Certainly, they had been permitted a small participation in the early Games, but it was strictly tokenism. Such voices as those of the Pope and de Coubertin himself had spoken against the inclusion of events for women. That females could play pit-a-pat tennis while dressed in ankle length skirts was accepted in a condescending manner by society, but most certainly females

PROGRAMME

JULY 1932

CANADIAN OLYMPIC TRIALS

HAMILTON, ONTARIO.

could not sweat! They might "glow" perhaps, but nothing more.

The 1928 Olympics put an end to that notion. A woman slamming out of the start of a 100 m dash could not do it in ankle length skirts and a woman running an 800 m race had to do more than "glow". Society in general may not have liked this change in women, but the change was there to stay.

The great depression that began in 1929 was another enormous force that wrought changes everywhere. After the affluence of the twenties, the plunge into the depression threatened athletics and the Olympic Games. Fortunately, although corners were cut, the quality of the Games in the thirties continued to be high. In the 1932 Olympiad in Los Angeles, a fantastic number of track records were set despite the gloomy predictions that reduced budgets would force many athletes to be left home. In actual fact, most countries applied stringent qualifying times and distances to their athletes and thus sent only their very best. The result was that although the number of entries was down, quality was up. This increase in quality might be attributed in part to the fact that many people without jobs had a staggering amount of time on their hands. What better way to employ that time, if you were an athlete, than to practice!

And how did Canada fare in this between-the-wars period? Canada reflected the times. There were two gold medals in 1920; four in 1928; two in 1932; and one in 1936. The two gold medals in 1920 were won by a boxer born in the US and trained in Canada, and a hurdler born in Canada and trained in the US! Of the four gold medals won in 1928, one was taken by Ethel Catherwood in the high jump; another by the women's 400 m relay team; and two were won by Percy Williams in the 100 and 200 m dashes. In 1932 Duncan McNaughton won Canada's last gold medal in track and field when he won the high jump, and "Lefty" Gwynne won Canada's last gold medal in boxing. In 1936, Canada's last gold medal until 1952 was won in canoeing by Francis Amyot.

Williams is by far the most outstanding of Canadian Olympic gold medal winners. His exploits did a great deal for the furtherance of athletics in Canada, for they gave credence to the ability of Canada to produce a world beater. Despite the overpowering influence of the US, Williams had been trained totally and completely in Canada and had resisted all offers to go to the States. He was a Canadian product and it gave Canadians, especially athletes, a great sense of pride and accomplishment to know that he was completely Canadian.

With the advent of World War II, athletics on the world scene went into hibernation. Canada's athletes, like those of other nations, became soldiers. Athletic technique, coaching and the expansion of facilities were put aside. Canada's production of gold medals has never reached the heights it did in the sixteen years and five Olympiads from 1920 to 1936.

1920 110m Hurdles
Earl Thomson
The Natural

The world was still reeling in the aftermath of World War I when the 1920 Olympics were held in Antwerp, Belgium. Longstanding animosities between nations were difficult to bury, and the war had made many people cynical as well. There was even a movement to abolish the Marathon as inhumane. To top everything, the *London Daily Express* carried an editorial which said, in part:

". . . We are bored with the Olympics. They are a waste of money and injure the spirit of sportsmanship without having any good effect on the relations of one people with another. Let us play the games and scrap the Olympics."

Yet, for all the difficulties and despite the fact that there were only three thousand athletes from twenty-seven countries "to compete in chivalrous spirit for the glory of sport", the Antwerp Games were vital for the reestablishment of the Olympics which had not been held since 1912.

When the monumental size of the financial and political obstacles that the Games had to overcome is considered, the 1920 Olympics have to be judged successful. Unfortunately, only one of Canada's ten-man Olympic team matched the success of the Olympics. His name was Earl "Tommy" Thomson – Gold Medallist, 110 m hurdles.

Unlike many of Canada's other gold medallists, Thomson's road to the Olympics was easy. He was a highly gifted athlete with an international reputation, and the Canadian Olympic committee eagerly sought him out.

Earl J. Thomson was raised in the Pasadena and Long Beach area of California and quickly became known as a great performer. In 1915, he won the State high school title in the high hurdles and discus throw, and tied for first in the high jump. In the same year, he won a match hurdles race against Fred Kelly, US Olympic champion of 1912.

By any standards, these achievements were outstanding but for Thomson they meant even more. Only six years before he had been given up for dead.

Tommy Thomson lived on a farm and like most farm boys, he hunted. During one hunt, when he was

fourteen, he stepped down from the buggy in which he was riding, and accidentally discharged a loaded shotgun into the left side of his chest. The massive wound appeared fatal. A four-hour emergency operation patched him as well as possible, but the doctors had little hope for his recovery. A surgeon, arriving at the hospital the next morning asked "What time did the young lad die?" To his surprise he was told that Thomson was very much alive.

That near-tragic accident kept Thomson out of training for about two years, but when he came back, he came back with a vengeance. Instead of returning to his chores on the family farm after school, he took part in baseball games, and above all, track and field events.

He often said in later years that his all-round training after school was worth all the punishments he received at home for neglecting his farm work.

It certainly stood him in good stead many years later when he was captain of the "Big Green"

track team at Dartmouth. In many dual meets, the 6 foot, 3 inch, 195-pound Thomson would be a one-man track team. He frequently won low hurdles, high hurdles, shot-put, broad jump, discus, hammer, javelin, 220, and pole vault in the same meet! His best height in pole vaulting was 10 feet, 6 inches; the current Olympic record was about 12 feet. His athletic prowess did not stop there — in summers, he was a lifeguard, and much later an assistant coach of swimming at Yale University!

The tall, raw-boned Thomson was born in the small community of Birch Hills near Prince Albert, Saskatchewan, in 1895. His parents had farmed in the area, but moved to California when Earl was eight for the sake of his mother's health. John Thomson, Earl's father, never gave up the hope of returning to Canada, and so did not become an American citizen. Consequently, Earl, too, was a Canadian when the 1920 Olympics came along. Since he was not eligible for the American team, although he was the best hurdler in the country, a special invitation was sent to him by the Canadian team organizers.

Thomson was not unknown in Canada. In 1916, Thomson left college to join the Royal Canadian Air Force as an observer. While in training at Beamsville, Ontario, he represented his station in an RCAF track meet. The one-man track team came through with five firsts and a second.

Fifteen hundred spectators attended the Olympic trials in Montreal and saw Thomson qualify for

Thomson and a Canadian team official at the Olympic trials held in Montreal, 1920.

the 110 m hurdles, the high jump, and the 400 m hurdles. His very presence gave the small, young Canadian team a measure of confidence. At twenty-five years of age, Thomson was sophisticated, capable and confident. Because of his hunting accident, he was older than most other athletes, but his maturity helped make him a leader.

The Olympics opened in war-torn Antwerp with the usual amount of acrimony. Great Britain gave notice that it would withdraw from future Olympics; the Swedish trainer resigned; the US committee dis-

qualified their world record holder in the triple jump for not meeting his curfew, and when two US boxers were suspended as well, the US athletes held a protest meeting on the eve of the Games threatening to withdraw. But the Olympics opened on time with the traditional parade.

The Canadian team was lead by hammer thrower Archie McDiarmid carrying a bare flag pole. No one had thought to supply a flag!

Thomson was entered in the 110 m hurdles in a total field of twenty-six entrants. In the preliminary heats, he ran against Barron of Philadelphia, and since the first two were to place, Thomson eased up at the finish and came second. In separate semifinal heats both Barron and Thomson equalled the Olympic record of 15 s set in 1908. The final was conceded to be between them.

The 110 m hurdles final had six contenders. Three were Americans, including the strong challenger, Barron. As they milled at the starting line, Thomson was relaxed and confident despite a minor muscle pull in his thigh which he had suffered earlier. Barron, beyond a terse "good luck", avoided looking at him, and with the others continued doing high kicks and jogging. Thomson swung his powerful loose-jointed legs over the first hurdle once or twice and then settled at the line to await the start.

At the gun, the entire group broke away swiftly. In quick stepping flight they soared gracefully over the first hurdles. By the third hurdle, Barron had taken a slight lead over Thomson. At the 50 m mark Thomson had regained the lost ground and began to draw away. His flawless, flowing style shot him forward. He skimmed so close to the hurdles it seemed he couldn't help but hit them. This perfect style gave him a distinct advantage and he finished a full 2 m in front of Barron. Thomson had won the gold medal and set a new world and Olympic record of 14.8 s! The record would stand for eleven years, a great tribute to Earl Thomson's great skill.

When the medals were presented, Thomson mounted the podium prepared to stand under the Red Ensign of Canada. The initial embarrassment of the officials at the opening parade was compounded when they realized there was no Canadian flag to hoist aloft. They quickly secured a British flag and raised it instead while Thomson had his gold medal placed around his neck. It was fortunate that the officials did not fly a US flag (as well they might have considering Thomson's background) for the US, probably as a backlash from the war, was very unpopular among the spectators who cheered lustily whenever an American lost a race.

Earl Thomson continued his love

Earl Thomson at the start of his thirty-seven-year career as head coach of Navy at Annapolis.

affair with track after retiring from competition. He became a coach, first at his Alma Mater, Dartmouth, and then at West Virginia and finally was made head coach of Navy at Annapolis. He coached there for thirty-seven years and in that period produced an amazing one hundred and fifty victories against only sixty-seven losses. In the 1943–46 period his midshipmen won nineteen consecutive meets, three ICAAA titles, and the 1945 NCAA championship.

Thomson was to earn many plaudits in his career as a coach, one of them being chosen to coach the Marine team at Camp Pendleton, California, after he retired from the naval academy. One of his athletes, Billy Mills, won the Olympic gold medal in the 10 000 m race in 1964.

Yet, even in his coaching Thomson had an obstacle to overcome. His hearing was damaged when he was in his thirties and he gradually became deaf. With grace and effortless good humour he accepted this burden and learned not only to live with it, but to function effectively in a demanding career.

Earl J. Thomson was, in the words of his wife, "a world champion of a man."

1920 Welterweight Boxing Albert Schneider Canada's Lend-Lease Boxer

Could an American athlete win an Olympic gold medal for Canada? Not today, perhaps, but in 1920 it did happen. Albert "Happy" Schneider, a twenty-three-year-old American boxer living in Montreal, represented Canada in Antwerp in the VII Olympiad and won the Welterweight Championship.

Boxing was included in the Antwerp Olympics for the first time since 1908. As a sport, it had fallen into disrepute because of its connection with unsavoury elements in society. Boxing had been a form of saloon entertainment, and had gained an infamous reputation from gambling and rigged fights. During the war, however, the military realized that boxing was a good way to instil military aggressiveness into troops while providing a fitness program at the same time. It was widely encouraged in the allied armies, and in the interallied games it was a major feature of the competitions. Its increasing popularity among the troops spread to the civilian population as well, and it became an international favourite once more.

Schneider came to Montreal from Cleveland when he was still an infant and retained his American citizenship. As he grew up, he became especially interested in athletics, and excelled at two completely different sports — boxing and water polo.

At the time of the Antwerp Olympiad, twenty-three-year-old Schneider was the Canadian welterweight amateur champion.

The opening ceremonies were

68

appropriately serious. They had been preceded by a Solemn Mass and a *Te Deum* in the cathedral where Cardinal Mercier had delivered an oration in memory of soldier-athletes who had fallen during the Great War. Every nation at the Olympics was represented at the service by a military delegation! Thus, after the athletes had all paraded into the stadium, it was understandable that a salute of cannon fire should be added to the ritual. Several hundred frightened pigeons were then released "to carry the news to all countries concerned."

The Canadian contingent to Antwerp did not travel as a group. Since boxing was to be held rather late in the program, the track team and swimmers departed first and it was they who took part in the opening parade.

When the boxing team arrived later they were a little wide-eyed at it all. Under the rules, each country was allowed two boxers plus a reserve man in each of the eight weight classes. Most of the ten nations competing in boxing did not send a twenty-four-man team because of the obvious financial burden it would create, but Britain, USA, France, Belgium and Denmark did. Canada's team consisted of only eight men as there was no Canadian heavyweight of international calibre, but despite their meagre numbers, the Canadian boxers finished third overall; Schneider winning and Cliff Graham, a flyweight, placing second.

The newspaper accounts of the Canadians in the Olympics that filtered back to Canada were very sparse. There were apparently no Canadian reporters assigned to cover the Olympics, and only an occasional line told of the Canadian team's fortune. Most of the coverage was about the US track and field team, intended for the US but picked up and printed verbatim by the Canadian papers. (One Quebec newspaper even listed Earl Thomson's victory in the hurdle race as a US win despite the fact that Thomson had won the Olympic track and field trials in Montreal only a few months previously.)

Despite this lack of public support those who knew Schneider best – people like Eugene Brosseau, a professional boxer who had helped coach him – knew that his nickname "Happy" reflected his temperament. At a party held in his honour shortly before his departure for the Olympics, Schneider's friends had presented him with gifts. He replied to this honour in his simple, good-natured way by a short speech.

"Fellows, you can depend on me to do my best, and if my best is better than the other fellow's best, then I will bring home the bacon."

Such a steady person would stand up well to the rigors of his first international competition.

The Sunday the boxing preliminaries began was stormy. As Schneider and his seven teammates entered the boxing hall they felt sure the humidity and heat would be a factor in the matches. Fortunately, the Olympics' organizers had scheduled all the secondary events around what is still con-

sidered the main attraction, track and field. This meant the boxing preliminaries were held in the morning, and the finals at night; the coolest times of the day.

After drawing a bye in the first round of matches, Bert faced four successive opponents. Each match consisted of three three-minute rounds and a final four-minute round. The officials consisted of two judges and a referee – the latter, under the rules of the time, outside the ring. The tournament was on a single elimination basis. There was no room for mistakes. "Happy" Schneider, who had never lost a bout as an amateur, would have to be constantly alert, and make the best use of every resource he possessed.

The first of his four opponents was Thomas of South Africa. Within seconds of the opening bell he had Thomas in trouble on the ropes. Schneider's heavy arms and shoulders delivered solid punishment that kept Thomas on the defensive for the rest of the match, and Schneider won a unanimous decision.

On Monday morning, Schneider's "buzz-saw" style worked to perfection and he knocked out Steen of Norway in the second round, to advance him to the semifinals. In the other half of the draw, Colberg of the US was the winner. Thus, two American citizens would be meeting in the semifinals for two different countries.

This strange circumstance happened in all innocence. Schneider, as a young boxer, was not even aware that the sport was on the

Olympic program. The Olympics were not as well known to the general public in those days and the Olympic rules were even less familiar. The rule that any athlete representing a country in the Olympics must be a citizen of that country was completely unknown to Schneider. No one on Canada's Olympic Committee thought to check his citizenship and no other country thought to question his status. When Schneider won the Welterweight Championship of Canada and, later, the Olympic trials, it was obvious that he be considered for the Olympic team. The stage was now set for an American to beat an American.

The US team had a full complement of twenty-four boxers so Colberg had a variety of sparring partners. He also had the advantage of knowledgeable corner people to instruct and help him between rounds. "Happy" Schneider was going to be hard pressed.

Right from the opening seconds, Schneider's power was evident. He barged through Colberg's classic defence and muscled him back. With his chin tucked safely behind his shoulder, and his powerful arms pumping, Schneider quickly gained points with his sledgehammer blows. Advancing, attacking, he wore the more experienced Colberg down. The great advantage "Happy" had in hitting power enabled him to bore into Colberg in the last round, knowing that the American had no strength left to land a knockout punch. It was only Colberg's versatility in combinations and defences that kept him on his

feet. The match ended in another victory for Schneider. He had advanced to the finals.

Only one of his teammates had done as well – little 112-pound Cliff Graham, one of two flyweights on the Canadian team. The other four who had reached the semifinals had been eliminated. It remained for either Graham or Schneider to win a gold medal.

On Tuesday evening Schneider stepped into the ring to meet Alex Ireland of Great Britain in the gold medal match. He waited calmly in his corner waiting for Ireland to emerge from the gloom outside the ring. Ireland appeared with his robe draped over his shoulders. His seconds held the ropes apart and he stepped gracefully between them and stood in his corner.

"Happy" Schneider examined him calmly. Ireland was not as heavily built in the shoulders as Schneider was, but he had powerful legs giving him great spring, and a very fast left hand. His unmarked features spoke of his boxing skill, and his rippling muscles his superb physical condition.

This was to be a match between a classic boxer and a puncher. The contrast in styles and body types made the match, especially for the Olympic Welterweight Championship, a fight promoter's dream.

As the bell sounded, Schneider moved to his opponent and slipped a left lead. A lightly thrown right followed that grazed Schneider's chin. He moved forward. Ireland threw several stabbing left hands that rained on Schneider's shoulders, head and arms. He continued

71

to move forward. Ireland peppered him with a flurry of lefts and rights and then tied him up, spun him around and danced back to the centre of the ring. Schneider looked slow and awkward. Thirty seconds into the match and he had not yet thrown a punch!

He advanced again determined to trap the weaving Ireland. Taking ten more light punches, Schneider manoeuvred his opponent into a corner and his left shot out like an adder's tongue to connect solidly to Ireland's body. This pattern was repeated over and over. Schneider taking dozens of light punches, especially left-hand jabs and hooks, to land one or two solid body blows. The round ended with both men glistening with sweat under the harsh glare of the ring lights; Schneider's face and shoulders reddened by the stinging blows of Ireland's left, and Ireland's ribs and abdomen blotched with his opponent's heavy punches. The round went to Ireland.

In the second round, Ireland maintained his strategy of keeping the battle at long range. Schneider pursued him relentlessly, only to have his attack stopped by a clinch in which he was spun around at the last moment. But Schneider never gave up; the pace was beginning to tell. Toward the end of the round, Bert managed to trap Ireland in a corner and sink two lefts to the chest forcing Ireland to lower his hands. A heavy right crashed into the side of Ireland's head and he flung himself into a clinch, hanging on desperately. The bell sounded to end the round.

The judges ruled it a draw.

Round three saw Ireland even more cautious. He flicked his left and danced away, rarely following his long jab with a right-hand punch. Schneider glided after him, shoulders hunched, his chin held low. Twice he trapped Ireland against the ropes, landing a heavy barrage of blows, wasting some in his eagerness, but pummelling Ireland's arms, shoulders, ribs, and head. It was Ireland's classic form which saved him as he ducked and feinted and darted back to ring centre.

Both men were now arm weary. It had been a telling and heavy fight. Both were grateful when the bell sounded; they threw their arms around each other briefly and then retired to their respective corners to await the verdict. Chests heaving, they looked up as the referee beckoned them to the side of the ring. They were informed that the match had ended in a draw! Incredibly, the referee now asked them to fight one more round to settle the match.

Three extra minutes for a gold medal. "Happy" Schneider thought back to his friends in Montreal. He did not want to let them down. As the bell sounded, he took a deep breath and lunged to the centre of the ring determined that this round would see him win it all.

Schneider carried the fight to Ireland immediately. Pumping lefts and rights, he forced the English favourite to cover up. He forced him to the ropes. Twice, it appeared he would put Ireland down, and twice the wily boxer eluded him. Ireland's blows by this time were little more than insect bites. Bert's body attack combined with the intense tempo of the match had reduced Ireland's strength to the point where he would throw a brief flurry of blows and then clutch. Finally, the long match ended. A brief consultation between referee and judges and the match was awarded to Schneider. His ready smile had never been larger. He was a gold medal winner!

Like many Olympic boxers, Schneider turned professional soon after winning his gold medal, and fought about seventy-five fights. He was not, unfortunately, given very good management, and retired from the sport after only a few years. His happy disposition stayed with him however, as did his gold medal victory — one of only two boxers from Canada who ever managed such a feat at the Olympics.

1928
100 m, 200 m
Percy Williams
The World's
Fastest Human

The vibrant "roaring twenties" were coming to a close, and the great depression of the 30's was just around the corner. For the thousands of spectators and participants in Amsterdam for the summer Olympics of 1928, however, the atmosphere was heady and full of life. The Olympics had caught hold of the imagination of the world, and the promotion and media coverage were better than ever. The squabbles that marked almost every previous Olympics were far fewer in 1928 than at any other time.

To the pleasure-loving twenties crowd, the hero of the Games was Paavo Nurmi. The great Finnish distance runner with the stolid features and barrel chest simply ran everyone into the ground, machine-like and without flair. He had won two gold medals in the 1500 and 5000 m runs in 1924, and was favoured in the 10 000 m run in 1928. The crowd, however, would willingly take a more compatible hero if he were offered.

Although he had equalled the Olympic record in the 100 m race during the Olympic team trials in Hamilton, Percy Williams was merely a face in the crowd of eighty-seven aspirants in the 100 m event. The overwhelming favourites were the Americans who had won six of the previous eight Olympic events. With such a formidable field none except a faithful few felt that the 126-pound Williams posed much of a threat. Indeed, Williams was by far the smallest of all the sprinters – it was no wonder that the fun-loving crowd took Percy to their hearts.

Williams' coach, Bob Granger, prepared him for his race in what was, for that day, a unique fashion. Williams almost never ran a time trial! Instead, he ran against an opponent. If Granger could not supply someone swift enough to challenge Williams, it was arranged for his running mate to be given up to a ten yard advantage. The experts felt this accounted for Williams' ability to "shift gears". He would start very fast, settle into a smooth even pace, and then shift once more into a burst that invariably carried him to victory over the last few yards.

Granger had trained Williams in Vancouver; this made the victories especially sweet since most of Canada's track and field heroes went to US colleges. Their accomplishments were felt to be the products of their American training rather than their own abilities.

Such was not the case with "Peerless Percy" as he came to be known. He was born, raised, schooled and trained in Vancouver.

In the Hamilton Olympic trials in June, 1928, Percy became the darling of the crowd by equalling the world record in the 100 m, while beating a field of top-rated, often American college-trained runners. His time was 10.6 s. He also won the 200 m in a time of 22 s. Percy Williams was named to the Olympic team at age nineteen!

In Amsterdam, things began in earnest for Williams. In four days he ran eight pressure-filled races, winning six and placing second in two.

In his first heat of the 100 m, Percy won easily in the slow time of 11 s. This, of course, was consistent with his approach of running against the man rather than against a clock. In the second heat he was forced to run his fastest race of the Games, equalling the Olympic record of 10.6 s.

In the semifinal the next day, Percy got off to a bad start and Coach Granger thought it was all over. Caught back on his haunches as the gun sounded, Williams started the race looking at the backs of seven other athletes disappearing up the track. He rocketed out of the starting holes (no blocks were used), and caught and passed all but McAllister, the American who in turn tied the Olympic record. Second place qualified Williams for the final. By now, the diminutive Canadian sporting the red maple leaf on his chest had captured the fancy of the spectators.

The next day Williams lined up for the final with McAllister and Wykoff of the USA, Lammers of Germany, London of Great Britain and Legg of South Africa. The men shifted continuously, their faces set and grim. When the gun went off, 80 000 people would watch to see who would be the world's fastest human.

Williams appeared a child among men, crouched as he was beside the 200-pound London. The tension was too great. Legg of South Africa broke and the entire field jogged off down the track bouncing and shaking their arms to alleviate the tightness. Back into the starting pits once more. The gun was up. Once again, a break. Wykoff of the USA this time. Williams jogged back and forth appearing very cool. His powerful legs seemingly outsized for his small body. Again, everything was in readiness. The gun was up. This time a good start.

Williams made a perfect break from the holes coming out in front with London just inches behind him. Williams settled into his mid-race pace and found Legg and Wykoff flanking him; but the red maple leaf stayed out in front. London came up and made a tremendous challenge, but Williams simply shifted into his famous finishing explosion of speed and crossed the line. He had won the gold and the title of "World's Fastest Human".

After the race Williams was mobbed by the ecstatic Canadian team and carried aloft around the infield. The American coach was among the first to offer his congratulations. The crowd took to

Williams like a parent to a child. The British were jubilant at the Empire carrying off the honours of the day. Here and there Scotsmen, Englishmen and Irishmen, in company with Australians and South Africans, could be seen arm-in-arm looking for the Canadians to offer congratulations.

Williams' effort astounded the experts, and it was the worst setback the US had ever experienced in the sprints. London of Great Britain had placed second and Hammers of Germany third, so the best place finish for the US was out of the medals. General Douglas McArthur, president of the US Olympic Committee, felt constrained to make a public statement to the effect that Williams was the greatest sprinter the world had ever seen.

Now, flushed with victory, Williams faced the prospect of at least two more gruelling days of competition. He was entered in the 200 m race and in the relay. The Canadian officials approached Williams with the option of scratching from the 200 m race after his stupendous win in the 100. Williams quietly insisted that he would run.

So began the whittling process for the 200 m. Percy used his flowing style to advantage in winning the first two heats. He tied the Olympic record in the second heat with a time of 21.6 s. Many had predicted that the frail-looking Williams would never last through the preliminaries of the 200 m race. The task looked too gruelling, the competition too tough. Paddock, the American who won the 100 m in 1920, declared, "It seemed impossible for that skinny little sprinter to do it!" Yet the deceptive Williams kept running and winning against the best in the world. The crowd adored him and every accolade heaped upon his narrow, boyish shoulders was accepted in a quiet and gentlemanly way.

In the 200 m final, the spectators sensed the drama. Williams could become a double winner. It would be the only such track and field victory Canada had ever achieved in the Olympics. The endless shifting movement betrayed the tension in the runners. Rangeley from Britain and Kornig from Germany were two powerful runners determined to keep Williams from the gold. The gun was up, and the field broke cleanly with Williams once

Saluting the flag after the 100 yards final at the 1930 British Empire Games. In one race Williams tore a thigh muscle and although he won that race, he was never able to compete at his old speeds again.

Authors' Collection

more getting a good start. He and Kornig were leading and running stride for stride for the first 150 m. Williams then went into his famous "shift" and drove hard to the finish line. The amazed Kornig seemed to hesitate as the frail youngster flashed ahead of him. Williams was too fast to be caught. He finished in a time of 21.8 s.

Once again the stands went wild. Maybe here was an alternate hero to the mechanical, stolid Nurmi. This modest Canadian kid had done what no world expert thought possible of him – he had won a double sprint victory at the Olympics!

There remained only the relay to be run. The Canadian officials asked Percy if he wanted to withdraw from the race in view of his already impressive production of medals. He felt he should see his task through and remained on the team. Chief of the Canadian delegation, J. P. Mulqueen, reported to the ever-inquiring press that Percy was sleeping like a baby in preparation for the relays on Saturday. When the relays came, they were an anticlimax. A poor baton exchange disqualified the team. This performance did not dim Williams' two gold medals one bit. He was ready, however, to return to Canada.

The return was a triumph likened to those presented for the winners of the Ancient Games. In every city in which he stopped, Williams and his mother (who met him in Quebec) were fêted and praised. In Montreal,

Percy Williams' Vancouver Victory Parade

Mayor Houde presented Williams with a gold watch from the city of Montreal. In Hamilton, scene of his record-tying performance in the trials, a motor parade was arranged and thousands of fans paid homage to him in Dundurn Park. The city

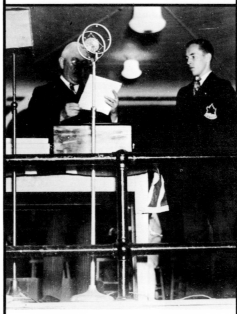

THE GLOBE AND MAIL, TORONTO

Percy Williams being received by the Mayor of Toronto at the bandstand of the CNE.

presented Percy with a silver tea service at a civic banquet in the evening. In Winnipeg, Williams was literally engulfed by the crowd as he descended from the train. A sea of hands reached out to touch and congratulate him. The city presented him with a bronze statue of a winner at the mark, and a silver cup.

Finally in mid-September, Williams reached Vancouver. The

reception was the largest ever seen. People mobbed the train, and the motorcade down Granville Street showed him off to tens of thousands of cheering Vancouverites. In the parade were 3000 school children and several bands. At the reception in Stanley Park, Williams, as befitting the times, was presented with a sporty blue Graham Paige automobile and a trust fund of $14 000 for his education. Coach Granger received $500. It was a highly charged and emotional moment for the crowd and for Percy Williams.

Percy Williams continued to compete with an eye to the 1932 Olympics in Los Angeles. In 1930 he set a new world record in the 100 m at Toronto with a time of 10.2 s. At the trials for the 1930 British Empire Games, Williams was flying down the track in Hamilton when he tore a muscle in his thigh. Although he won the race, and continued to compete, he never could run at his all-out maximum again. The easy flowing style was there, but the hard finishing burst was gone.

In the 1932 Olympics, showing just flashes of his old abilities, Williams was able to manage a fourth place in the 100 m. It was a tribute to his tremendous capacity as well as his courage that he should finish so high with such a serious injury.

The saga of "Peerless Percy" was over, but those moments of glory live on in the memory of thousands of Canadians. All of the elements were combined to make those few seconds among the most outstanding in Canada's Olympic history.

Public Archives of Canada

1928 High Jump Ethel Catherwood The Saskatoon Lily

The 1928 Olympics were raucous and noisy. The crowds trying to get into the Amsterdam Stadium were so large that the Finnish team was forced to clamber over the wall to get onto the track for the opening day parade because the entrance was barred by an unruly mob of gate crashers.

The crowd was all the more enthusiastic because of a controversy that had raged just prior to the Games. The Pope had condemned the proposed inclusion of track and field events for women claiming the events, especially the 800 m run, were not suitable for females! The International Olympic Association took it to a vote. Canada voted against the inclusion of women's events, but women prevailed on the basis of a majority vote. With women's track and field events included for the first time, a special flavour was added to that "glamour event" of the Olympics.

Females had been permitted in swimming and tennis competition as early as 1908, but it wasn't until the Roaring Twenties that they were permitted to compete in track and field. Even the founding father of of the Olympics, Baron de Coubertin, was against their inclusion. He cited the early Greek taboos against women competitors and stated, "It is against my wishes they have been admitted to an increasing number of contests." He protested in vain.

The reigning queen of the 1928 Olympic Games was Her Majesty Queen Wilhelmina of the Netherlands, but without a doubt, the reigning princess was Canada's Ethel Catherwood, the "Saskatoon Lily". Cool and poised, the most photographed girl at the Games won a gold medal in the high jump and nearly broke her own world's record in the process.

Although Ethel was listed as a Toronto girl, her real home was Saskatoon. She had been persuaded to move east in order to train more intensively for the Olympics. It would appear, however, that most of her success was due to her early training for she had leaped as high as 5 feet, 2 inches in 1926, two years before her gold medal. The height of her winning jump in Amsterdam was 5 feet, 2.625 inches.

Catherwood had an almost dis-

passionate approach to competition. A good example of it was seen during the Ontario trials held to determine which Ontario girls would go to the Dominion trials in Halifax. During the high jump, Ethel performed with her usual calm air. When the bar reached 5 feet and all her opposition had been defeated, she stopped jumping. She did not wish to try for a record. Some coaches today would have applauded her action feeling that there are only a limited number of absolute maximum performances in any one athlete. Using them up in a local meet might mean losing an important one.

There was a certain naivety and lack of sophistication concerning sport in those days. This was especially true in Canada. Very few knew what record times and distances were, and except for a few observant people such as Joe Griffiths from the University of Saskatchewan, Ethel Catherwood might have gone unheralded on the prairies. Griffiths, a member of the physical education department at the University, realized that a jump of 5 feet could possibly win the Olympics even though no one could really say what the world record was because records were not accurately kept. Virtually any female who leaped about that height could claim it as a record and then wait to be challenged. Griffiths, however, felt that Ethel had great potential that should be developed.

The potential should have been there, too, if one believes in genetic endowment. Ethel's brother was a

fine athlete and was dash champion of Saskatchewan. Her father was also an outstanding athlete and the family ties in athletics went back to Ned Hanlan, Canada's premier oarsman of the late 1800's whose statue graces Toronto's CNE waterfront.

With that background, Ethel seemed fated to do well in almost everything. Indeed, Griffiths challenged her with more than jumping. He entered her in the discus and javelin. She responded by breaking the Canadian record in 1928 by 12 feet with a toss of 118 feet, 8 inches. The javelin throw was not included in the program for the 1928 Olympiad, and Ethel did not have a chance to show her ability internationally in this event.

Catherwood reached her peak in some very good company. There were five other Canadian girls who made up the Canadian entry in the first Olympic track and field meet for women. Between them, the "Matchless Six," as the newspapers called them, amassed enough points to win that division of the Olympics against the other forty-one nations entered.

Ethel's Olympic medal came late in the Games. The world had already been astounded by Percy Williams' double sprint victory. The US had been shocked by their own disappointing showing in track. Canada's wrestlers and rowers were doing well. The "Matchless Six" had been performing up to their pre-Games billing. The effect of all of this was such that the fans in the crowd often called to the Canadians, especially the girls,

"What are you going to win today?" Ethel's statuesque beauty and icy poise quickly made her a favourite with the crowd. Photographers pressed around at every opportunity, and there were rumours of a movie offer even before she won her medal. It did not ruffle the princess of the Games though, and the mob loved her for it all the more.

Her quiet confidence was probably bolstered by the fact that at the trials in Halifax she had jumped 5 feet, 3 inches. Thus, when she managed to place only seventeenth in the morning trials of the Olympic high jump, she was not too worried. A low profile in the early going is often the mark of a champion because it reduces the pressure that is bound to increase in the later stages of the competition.

The finals of the Olympic high jump event for women began at 2:00 p.m. Each contestant had to make a qualifying jump at 4 feet, 6 inches and all were successful. The day was chilly and damp, so Ethel did not remove her sweatsuit in the early part of the competition. Carefully hoarding her strength and determined to stay loose and warm, Ethel continued to jump in her warm-up clothes. At 5 feet she missed. Unperturbed on her second attempt, she waited until the last second before removing her sweatsuit and then cleared the bar easily. She, perhaps unwittingly, was out-psyching her opposition. If she could do nearly 5 feet in her sweat-

Ethel Catherwood using her modified scissors style in a 1927 competition at Toronto's CNE.

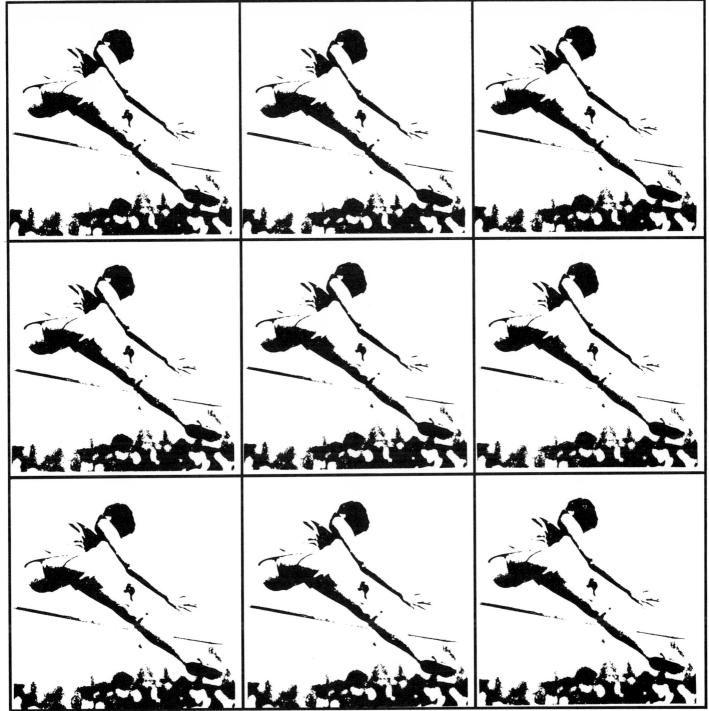

suit, what could she do unencumbered?

By this time, the opposition had dwindled to two – Gisolf of Holland and Wiley of the USA. Of the two, Wiley was thought to be the more dangerous. She was coached by Dick Landon who had won the Olympic high jump in 1920. When Mildred Wiley jumped 5 feet, 0.5 inches in training, Landon, like Griffiths, felt his charge had an excellent chance of winning. The tension increased tremendously for Ethel Catherwood when she looked over at Mildred Wiley and realized one slip, one mistake, and the gold medal could be snatched from her.

With the bar set at 5 feet, 3 inches, all three women were still in contention. Ethel had never been pressured like this before. Although she did not show it, her composure was beginning to crack. Like the champion she was, however, she rose to the occasion. On her first jump using her modified scissors style she sailed cleanly over the bar. Both her opponents failed. Ethel had won Canada's second gold medal of that day (the women's relay team won the other). A measure of the bar proved it had sagged below the 5 foot, 3 inch mark and thus it was not listed as a world but as an Olympic record. Catherwood had taken fewer than ten jumps in a contest that had lasted for three hours! It is a tribute to her cool, concentrated approach to the competition that she should win in such a fashion.

The jubilation in the Canadian camp at Ethel's success was almost as great as when Percy Williams had won his gold medals earlier. Even the stoic princess herself laughed and bounded around in ecstasy. Quickly, the Canadians hoisted her to their shoulders, and the most photographed girl at the Games was paraded before the screaming, waving crowd. The Canadians tallied their points and with Ethel's win they took the championship of the women's division even over the vaunted US girls. It was a great day for Canada and for Ethel Catherwood.

After a brief tour of England and France to compete in post-Olympic invitational meets, the "Matchless Six" left for home to a hero's welcome. They were eager to return.

On the way to Saskatoon, there were parades held to honour the women's team in Montreal, Toronto and Hamilton. Always, there were gifts from a grateful citizenry. The parade in Toronto was mammoth, and the city presented Ethel with a gold watch and a case of silver. But if her reception in those places caused excitement, it was nothing compared to the hysteria in Saskatoon.

The papers said her arrival at home caused more excitement than the town had seen since the signing of the 1918 Armistice. It was the largest reception in the city's history. Over two thousand people jammed the train station – a wild, scrambling, arm-grabbing mob. The bubbling enthusiasm of the crowd full of well-wishers eager to welcome the gold medallist infected Catherwood. She declared, "I'm more excited at getting home than at any time during my experience in Amsterdam." A statement that was certainly not going to cool the adoring people.

The entire student body of Ethel's high school, Bedford Road Collegiate, had marched to the station to meet her. They stood and listened while dignitaries from the Mayor to the President of the Elks Club paid tribute to Ethel. The Elks had sponsored her Toronto training and transportation to other centres for meets. The Mayor felt a proprietary interest in her as any good civic administrator would. He finally hit the high point of his speech. Catherwood's dream was to continue her piano study, for she was already fairly accomplished in that area, too. The Mayor presented her with a $3000 education trust fund. The money had all been raised locally, with $2000 coming from the city and $1000 from local clubs. Ethel received it with tact and grace and told her breathless audience that she would use the gift to continue her piano studies.

When questioned later about the rumoured Hollywood offers, Ethel would only say, "I'd rather gulp poison than try my hand at motion pictures." She did reiterate her intention of pursuing a business course in Toronto. Thus, one of the stellar members of Canada's 1928 world champion women's team ended her brief stay on the international stage. Her presence had come at a time when events like the Olympics were beginning to make the world an international community and her display of talent and charm helped make Canada a well-received part of it.

1928
400 m Relay
Bell, Cook, Rosenfeld & Smith
Women's Olympic Lib

In 1928, women's track and field events were included in Olympic competition for the first time. Male dominance of Olympic athletics declined quickly after that, even though the inclusion of women's athletics in the ninth Olympiad was made over the protests of the Pope and Baron de Coubertin, founder of the modern Olympics.

The miniscule team of six Canadian girls made the most of their debut into the international scene by winning the team title and capturing two gold medals, one silver, one bronze, one fourth place, and one fifth place.

Four of the girls, Fanny Rosenfeld, Ethel Smith, Florence Bell, and Myrtle Cook, shared a gold medal when they won the 400 m relay and set a new world record in the process.

Fanny Rosenfeld bounced and jogged on the cinder track. It was the last day of Olympic competition in Amsterdam. A few days earlier, she had lost the gold medal in the 100 m dash. A very close finish with Robinson of the USA had resulted in a judge's decision that had gone against Fanny. Her great competitive spirit was aroused. This time, her last chance, she was determined to take a gold medal.

Yet her determination was not without humour as well. Named the "life of the party", Fanny could keep her teammates loose and relaxed with an endless stream of jokes and a constantly cheerful approach to life. Fanny also happened to be one of the most talented female athletes in the world. She was later to be named Canada's female athlete of the half century.

At age 23, Fanny, a worker in a Toronto chocolate factory, held Canadian records in running long jump, standing long jump, discus

Fanny Rosenfeld with some of the trophies she won under the sponsorship of Patterson's Choclate Factory.

Alexandra Studio

and shot-put, as well as being an outstanding baseball player. Her distance in the discus during Olympic trials was 129 feet, 1 inch and the winning toss in Amsterdam was 130 feet.

Fanny dropped from the discus competition in order to concentrate on track events; she entered three events and placed in three events, breaking records in two of them! She was second in the 100 m, fifth in the 800 m (where she surpassed the existing world record) and now was ready to win gold. The starter calling the girls for the beginning of the 400 m relay final.

Fanny stood in her lane looking down at the footholds dug into the cinder track. This was the track where no records were expected because it had had to be relaid just ten days prior to the start of the Olympics. How wrong the predictions had been! Twelve records were set in the twenty-two men's events and new ones set in all five of the women's events.

The experts had been right about something else, though. Back in Canada they predicted the Canadian girls would do very well. Three of the girls advanced to the finals of the 100 m dash alone! All three were now in the final of the 400 m relay.

Their send-off had been terrific. The mayor of Toronto was one of the many well-wishers who had come down to the train to wish them good luck. Their chaperone, Alexandrine Gibb, had pampered and ushered them around like a mother hen. On the boat crossing to the Netherlands, Gibb had seen to it

that they had a daily workout in the gym, had eaten properly (no pop allowed) and had plenty of sleep (in bed by 10:30).

Awaiting the "get set" of the starter, Fanny could look down the track and see Ethel Smith, dressed in the rather controversial outfit the Canadian girls had chosen. Their shorts were daringly brief for the times and they had cut out the sleeves of their track shirts to give their arms more freedom of movement.

Ethel was another all-round athlete who played softball and basket-ball as well as holding the Canadian Women's title in the 200 m dash. In the 100 m final a few days earlier, Ethel had finished just a step behind Fanny Rosenfeld to take the bronze medal. In the Canadian finals in June, the order had been reversed with Ethel second and Fanny third. In her heat to gain the Canadian final, Ethel had had to defeat Rosa O'Neill, the defending North American record holder, and she did it in a great upset. Thus she was familiar with tough, down-to-the-wire competition. She was eager and ready to put everything into this last attempt at gold.

The rough cinders dug into Fanny Rosenfeld's hands as she waited for the gun. Yesterday this Canadian team had established a new world mark in the 400 m relay of 49.4 s and won their heat. Fanny was bursting to go. She was going to show the world how fast they really could run. A split second before the gun went off, Fanny broke. The runners were recalled and Fanny's

The 1928 Canadian team cheering in the stands of the Amsterdam Olympics.

90

name was taken. One more false start would disqualify the team. Only a few days before, Myrtle Cook, Canada's world record holder in the 100 m dash, had been thrown out of the final for having two false starts. Fanny was determined to take no chances. As the gun went up once more, she held back deliberately. The gun sounded and the runners exploded from their starting pits. Fanny was not among the leaders. She held steady a step or two behind the front runners as they approached the first exchange.

Ethel Smith looked over her shoulder at the rapidly nearing runners. She shifted her feet restlessly. She remembered the training each morning on the *Albertic* during their passage over to the Games, and before that, the weeks of training at the Canadian Ladies' Athletic Club in Toronto – training that brought funny looks to the faces of certain people who believed it unladylike. But at 21, Ethel was more than equal to the stares. She was here in Amsterdam at the Olympics and Fanny was approaching fast with the baton. In a wink of an eye she had it and was gone.

The baton Ethel carried up the track toward Florence Bell was something special. It had been presented to the girls by one of the premier track clubs in Canada, the Hamilton Olympic Club. Not only had the HOC presented the girls with the baton, they had given the Olympic Association $2800. The baton had been passed frequently on the deck of the *Albertic* in order that the girls be fully familiar with it. It was now on the most important journey it would ever make.

At 18, Florence Bell was the youngest on the team. She, too, in keeping with the versatility of the rest of the group, was not only a runner, but a Canadian Champion hurdler, a swimmer and a baseball player.

Florence had been very impressed by the opening parade and the special significance of the flag the girls had been given by the head of the Canadian delegation, P. J. Mulqueen. The flag was the one carried by the victorious Canadian ice hockey team at the 1924 Winter Olympics in Chamonix. It had a winning tradition and Mulqueen gave it to the girls to inspire them. It seemed to be working.

Ethel pounded up the track and inched past one of her competitors. She bore down on Florence like a fury. Florence turned and began sprinting. She felt the slap of that solid baton in her palm, wrapped her fingers around it tightly and shifted into high gear. She too, had something to prove.

In the first heat of the 100 m, Florence had been a victim of international stage fright. Her inexperience and youth worked against her and she got off to a bad start. She was eliminated in the first heat – the only Canadian girl to fail her first test. Now like a reprieve, she was being given a chance to show just what she could do. She tore down the track with a vengeance toward the compact form of Myrtle Cook. The baton jumped in her right hand as though pulling her along. She held the team in steady position in the middle of the pack.

Myrtle Cook

The baton. Myrtle Cook was worried about that thick cylinder of wood. Earlier in the Olympiad, the Canadian men's relay team had been disqualified for dropping their baton, and they had been one of the favoured teams. Would this happen to her? Myrtle Cook's hands were very small and Alexandrine Gibb had given her and the rest of the team daily drilling on the baton exchange to try to prevent any fumbling. But was it enough? Myrtle could not afford the emotional upset which would ensue if she dropped the baton. She was already the hard luck girl of the team. She had disqualified in the finals of the 100 m. Myrtle Cook, holder of the world's record of 12 s had not even been allowed to run the race.

Myrtle Cook was very sensitive. Even though she was the only member of the team with previous international experience, she was also the only one to cry from homesickness on the trip. She also sat at the side of the track and cried for half an hour at the time of her ejection from the 100 m. Her pride had been deeply hurt. However, she had strong self-discipline, and pulled herself together.

She watched as Florence Bell approached and adrenalin shot through her body. This was it. If Canada was to win a medal, Myrtle would have to run the last leg of the relay as she had never run before. Florence approached the passing zone and Myrtle started. All thoughts of fumbling the exchange had been driven from her mind. She began to accelerate

when she felt the hard slap of the wood in her palm and she jumped out of the pack. Within a few strides she had taken a slight lead and with 50 m to go had widened the gap. She flew down the track. All the pent-up frustration and emotion pumped her legs like pistons and she drove harder still as she approached the tape. She hit the finish line like a champion. She was out in front by several steps. Canada had won its fourth gold medal of the 1928 Olympics! The winning relay team broke its own world record by a full second with a time of 48.4 s.

The whole team jumped and ran crying and laughing and hugging one another. They were so ecstatic the photographers could not get them to stand still long enough for pictures. Photographers could wait! Right now they wanted to savour their moment. They had worked and sacrificed; they had been "unladylike" – and they had won. Their relay won them both a gold medal and the women's team title by a score of 34 points to 28 for runner-up USA.

A triumphant return home was

Myrtle Cook winning a preliminary heat. Though she held the Canadian 100 m record she was disqualified from the Olympic final by two false starts.

postponed while the girls participated in meets in France and England, and shopped in Paris. When they did reach Canada, the welcome was tumultuous. In Montreal, they were given a tour of the city and presented at a civic banquet. All the women received solid silver compacts from the city. In Toronto, their hometown, the wel-

come was awesome. A crowd of 200 000 jammed Union Station and Front Street to greet them on their arrival. The four-mile parade route was lined by another 100 000. When the motorcade of smiling athletes passed Patterson's chocolate factory, everyone was given a box of chocolates by Fanny Rosenfeld's admiring co-workers.

When the parade reached Sunnyside, a highly charged crowd sang "See Them Smiling Just Now" as the girls mounted the platform to be presented with a silver tea set each.

Later, the team attended a special reception in Hamilton for all the Olympic team members and were given special medals to mark the occasion.

The honours and gifts did not stop. Fanny Rosenfeld, for example, was presented with a new car by an admiring group of Toronto businessmen – an unheard-of luxury for a female factory worker.

Gradually, the excitement died, but their accomplishments lived on. The women's Olympic track and field program of five events grew to more than a dozen, and other events – such as canoeing and gymnastics – were expanded to include women. The impetus for such expansion came in large measure from the success of that first women's competition in the 1928 Olympics. And the most successful women's team of the year was Canada's.

Myrtle Cook stepping over the finish line to bring Canada a gold medal in the 400 m relay.

94

1932 High Jump Duncan McNaughton The Unwanted Canadian

The 1932 Olympics in Los Angeles were dominated by economics. The world-wide depression left money in short supply for such "luxuries" as the Olympics. Financial considerations made many countries adopt a policy of priorities whereby only those athletes with proven records were sent to the Games. Perhaps that accounted for the thirty-two new Olympic records that were set. Fortunately for Canada, there was an athlete who happened to be living in Los Angeles and could be included on the team at no additional expense. His name was Duncan McNaughton, and he won a gold medal.

Born in Cornwall, Ontario, raised in Kelowna, British Columbia and trained in California, McNaughton was virtually unmentioned by the Canadian sportswriters prior to the competition. Most of their prose was reserved for the political machinations particular to the Olympics and to accounts of "Peerless Percy" Williams who had electrified Canada with his double sprint victories in 1928. His new 100 yard world record in the Canadian championships of 1930 was finally accepted by the International Track and Field Association on the eve of the opening of the 1932 Olympic Games and Williams' practice runs were faithfully documented by a hopeful Canadian press. In the meantime, McNaughton, a face in the crowd of one hundred and thirty Canadian athletes, continued to practice the high jump. The newspapers made only a brief two-line mention of the fact that McNaughton and another Canadian, Portland, were jumping

95

well at 6 feet, 4 inches.

The newspapers then turned their attention to the political manoeuvrings going on. These included the deposition of the president of the Argentine Olympic Association which, according to one report, was done at gunpoint! The German Olympic Association accused the great Paavo Nurmi, the "Flying Finn", of receiving up to $500 for exhibition races. Nurmi denied everything and told reporters if he were barred, he would run anyway and make the winners of those races appear as fools. A newspaper reporter stated that "the Games without Nurmi is like history without Napoleon – he would mean $50 000 to the LA Games. In the real sense of the term Nurmi is not an amateur but neither were 99 per cent of the champions of the previous Olympics!" Quite an accusation to make in those days when it was also reported that the Los Angeles Games were $100 000 in the red as a result of the eastern USA reneging on some promised donations.

The Games, however, commenced in their inevitable fashion. Among the first events was the high jump. McNaughton, along with nineteen others from eleven different countries, began their contest at 2:00 p.m. under a hot California sun. The favourite was George Spitz who held the world indoor mark at 6 feet, 8.5 inches. The Olympic record set by Harold Osburne in 1924 was 6 feet, 6 inches. McNaughton's best height to that time was 6 feet, 4 inches.

McNaughton began winning high

Authors' Collection

school track championships at age fourteen. He taught himself to high jump by digging a pit back home in Kelowna, BC, and building high jump standards for it. He bought a Spalding text on jumping and began to produce the western roll, a style of jumping that persisted for about twenty-five years. Little did his high school coach, George Seivers, ever believe that Dunc would one day be challenging the world's best.

Despite McNaughton's obvious talents, he appeared at the Games only under sufferance. The Cana-

Three of the four high jump finalists: Duncan McNaughton, Simon Toribo and Robert Van Osdel. McNaughton and Van Osdel were university teammates but had to compete for different countries.

dian Olympic Association decided to leave him off their team because in the 1930 British Empire Games Trials, McNaughton had been disqualified for diving over the bar. Now in 1932, McNaughton was a student at the University of California and was competing for that institution. Under the tutelage of track coach, Dean Cromwell, and with the assistance of teammate Bob Van Osdel, McNaughton had steadily improved until he was almost the equal of Van Osdel although he had never beaten him. Despite the fact that McNaughton's "heights" were better that year

than those of anyone in Canada, the Olympic Committee rejected him.

The Olympic Committee itself was not beyond reproach. An editorial in the Toronto paper *The Globe,* of July 30, 1930, had this to say: "What Canada appears to need athletically are more competent ambassadors. Practically the same clique that mismanaged the 1928 team is again in charge in 1932."

It was felt by many people that selections to the team were not based solely on merit, but that favouritism and personal bias on the part of the Olympic Committee played a part. There were at least two other cases similar to McNaughton's. In one case, the mother of a girl swimmer prepared a formal protest over the non-selection of her daughter.

As Duncan McNaughton warmed up for the high jump event, 30 000 Canadians looked on in the huge stadium which held over 100 000 spectators. The tension was understandably high, but McNaughton's personality helped him through these crucial, pressure-filled few hours to the final jumps. His high school coach had described him as "a gangly boy with a keen sense of humour and a disposition like a million dollars." The favourite, Spitz, had been eliminated at 6 feet, 3 inches and by 6:00 p.m. there remained only McNaughton, Bob Van Osdel, his teammate from USC, Simon Toribio from the Philippines, and Cornelius Johnson of the USA.

All four men cleared the bar at 6 feet, 6 inches but failed at 6 feet, 7 inches. McNaughton's performance was already 2 inches higher than he had ever jumped before.

The officials went into a huddle to decide how to break the tie. The crowd, sensing the drama, riveted its attention on the jumpers even though the highly popular 100 m dash heats were being run at the same time. The officials' decision was to lower the bar to 6 feet, 6 inches and have the remaining four jumpers repeat their performances. As one after another the tiring athletes soared up and failed

on their first tries, the crowd gasped and moaned so loudly that the fourth heat for the 100 m was held up. The noise was distracting the runners and the starter.

On his second attempt, McNaughton faced the bar determined to succeed this time. His friend and rival Bob Van Osdel came over, looked Dunc in the eye and said, "Get your kick working and you will be over." The advice may not have helped specifically, but the spirit in which it was given made it worth more than mere analysis of technique. McNaughton stared again at the bar, and then was off on his approach. He stepped, kicked hard and was over! The crowds erupted in frantic cheers. The starter at the 100 m dash was also pleased that the high jump was finished at last.

Duncan McNaughton's gold medal snapped the USA's 36-year string of high jump victories and he hadn't even been selected to be on Canada's Olympic team!

McNaughton's magic moment in sports history was never matched by his subsequent performances. He continued to compete for only one year after his Olympic victory and never again achieved the standard he rose to on that day.

In World War II McNaughton joined the Royal Canadian Air Force and was awarded the DFC and bar. Subsequently, he became a petroleum geologist and in 1974 he was elected Vice-President of the American Association of Petroleum Geologists, the largest association of geologists in the world.

Boxer Horace "Lefty" Gwynne was a pure product of the depression – tough, aggressive, resourceful. He left school after grade eight to try to find a job – scarce for everybody but especially for someone who weighed 65 pounds.

Lefty's diminutive stature was used in two sports where small size could be an advantage – riding and boxing. In those hard depression years one was forced to make the best of every asset one had. There was no room for the luxury of error. So both Gwynne and his older brother decided to become jockeys. Horace signed a contract with Smallman of London and at the tender age of thirteen was sent to Cuba to apprentice as a jockey. His salary of $20 per month was sent to his mother and he was fed, clothed and housed by his employer.

When "Lefty" began to look like he might grow too large for a jockey, his father, who had once boxed, took him to Stokley's gym in Toronto to try to keep his weight down. Once at the gym, the elder Gwynne put his son in the care of a fight manager, Eddie Williams, who quickly recognized Lefty's potential and set to work bringing out the best in him.

One of Williams' first acts was to change Gwynne from a left-hand to a right-hand lead. He felt that in this way Gwynne would be able to get fights more easily since many boxers avoid left-handers. Lefty readily accepted Williams' decision and in about two weeks was as at home with a right-handed stance as he had been with a left-handed one.

1932 Bantam-weight Boxing Horace Gwynne From Jockey To Boxer

It was also Williams' idea to put Gwynne into the thick of boxing immediately. Today, it might be considered pushing too fast to begin a fight career by going into the ring with the Canadian champion! Such pressure too early in a career can have devastating results. Gwynne, however, proved to have the mettle necessary. He quickly gave both his sparring partners and his opponents as good as he got. He was matched in one sparring session with "Frenchy" Belanger who was world champion for a six-month period! Gwynne was seventeen at the time.

The training in Stokley's gym was not, however, Gwynne's first exposure to boxing. He had actually boxed at age four! Gwynne's father, a first generation Canadian from Wales, had gone back to the Old Country to join the British army just prior to World War I and had taken his family with him. By the end of the war, four-year-old Lefty and his older six-year-old brother Jack were giving boxing exhibitions for the troops, wearing great, pillowlike gloves. The pennies the soldiers threw to them were quickly gathered into jam jars and taken to mother. Mrs. Gwynne in turn gave Jack and Horace their spending money. This was not to be the only time in Lefty's career when his mother would handle his earnings!

As Lefty progressed at Stokley's gym, both he and his father set their sights on Los Angeles and, with only fifteen fights (including the Olympic trials) behind him, he was sent to the Olympics.

When Lefty reached Los Angeles

he was something of an enigma. He was well travelled, but naive. He had a lot of natural ability, but too little chance to develop it. Not only that, but all of his short career had been as a flyweight (112 pounds) until the Olympic trials when he became a bantamweight (118 pounds). In fact, the only matches he had fought as a bantamweight were the four it took to win the Canadian championships and trials in May, 1932.

Why did he move up a weight class? He had already been successful as a flyweight, having defeated Callura of Hamilton to win the Canadian championship in 1931 in London, Ontario. He changed weight classes because, incredibly enough, he did not feel he should lose weight and then box. Thus, when his poundage crept up to 116 pounds, rather than sweat off the meagre four pounds to become 112 again, he decided to move to the bantamweight class instead. Today many athletes lose 20 pounds or more in order to be in their proper divisions. It is unheard of to go "up" to a weight class. Competitors think only of going down. Not so with Lefty. He continued to train hard, eat plenty, and compete at 118 pounds even though he weighed only 116.

In those days, it was customary for Lefty and other jockeys to work at their track during summer only and in winter try to get some kind of factory job. Gwynne worked sporadically during winters, but always boxed and trained with great dedication; in the summer he worked hard as a jockey and did little or no boxing. But 1932 was different.

At his father's urging, young Lefty did not turn up at the track in the spring. Instead, he went to a farmhouse on Frenchman's Bay just west of Toronto and continued his boxing training. He spent nearly two months training three times a day without coaching or supervision. The young Gwynne knew what had to be done to become champion and he set to work with the head-down-here-I-come attitude that characterized all his fights.

Lefty's full-time training necessitated a large financial sacrifice for his father. Even though his room and board was only about $5 per week, this represented about a third of a bricklayer's weekly wage.

Lefty's training included 5 miles of road work interspersed with shadow boxing, an hour of punching light and heavy bags plus skipping, and then an hour of calisthenics. During his road work, Lefty would often take passers-by by surprise as he would suddenly stop to bob and duck and throw hooks at an imaginary opponent. The only disadvantage of the solitude of Frenchman's Bay was the lack of sparring partners.

His determination and training paid dividends after Gwynne won

the Canadian trials in May, 1932, when Oscar Pearson, physical director at the Toronto Central YMCA, invited Lefty to train for the Olympics at the Y. Pearson felt the publicity would be good for the institution, and Gwynne, of course, welcomed a place to work out that was free. Eddie Williams from Stokley's gym helped by providing sparring partners.

As the end of July approached, Gwynne was ready to go to Los Angeles to complete his training. He departed as one of a seven-man team, coached by Dennis White of Montreal.

When the first day of competition finally arrived, the entire Canadian team was ready for it. Gwynne awoke from a characteristically sound sleep and prepared to go to the boxing arena. Years later, when asked if he felt any anxiety about his first match with the Italian defending champion, Gwynne said that he felt no differently. However, this was explained by the fact that Gwynne never saw a draw sheet and did not know whom he would fight until he got to the arena. He neither scouted his opponents nor even bothered to watch them. His simplistic approach kept him calm and confident. He just went out and did his best — and that was good

enough for a gold medal.

In his first match against the Italian, Melis, his left hook piled up points in the first round and forced the Italian to come on stronger in round two. As Melis opened up, Lefty nailed him with a right to the chin that more or less decided the match. Melis weathered the third round, but Gwynne won the match.

In his second match, he faced his toughest opponent, Villeneuve of the Philippines. In the second round, Villeneuve caught Gwynne off balance and hit him with six straight punches. Tested for the first time, Gwynne reached quickly into his reserves. The hours spent in solitary roadwork, the jarring punches of his bigger, more experienced sparring partners, the bull-dog determination, and quick, natural ability — all were put into the flurry of punches Lefty mustered to regain control of the match. He was relentless and pursued his opponent with what the newspapers described as a "devastating broadside into the Filipino's middle." Lefty won and advanced to the final.

Gwynne's opponent in the final match was Hans Ziglarski, the German veteran who had finished second in the 1928 Olympics. He was a typical European boxer, a headlong rusher who threw over-hand rights and wild swinging lefts. Fighting him was, at times, like running into a circular saw. Gwynne could not afford to do a lot of long-range jabbing and fancy footwork; he had to punch.

And punch he did. He pulled up Ziglarski's first rush with sizzling jabs that snapped the German's head back and brought tears to his eyes. He then manoeuvred his opponent to the corners and kept him on the defensive by using a clubbing left hook and cross-fire rights.

In the second round, the nineteen-year-old Gwynne stopped Ziglar-ski's rush and then cornered him. A straight left flush on the jaw staggered his taller opponent and a hard right put him down. Ziglar-ski was up at the count of two, but his fight tactics were gone. He backpedalled furiously, and when-ever Gwynne caught him, he clinched desperately. He managed to hang on until the round's end, but lost many points for his poor performance.

The last round was anticlimactic. Ziglarski kept his distance with long-range ineffective jabs. As the fight ended, the crowd of six thou-sand stood and applauded the hardest punching fighter of the

Lefty Gwynne, thirty-seven years after his Olympic victory.

Games. Horace Lefty Gwynne had won his gold medal.

Before he left the arena, Gwynne had several offers to turn pro. Al-ways mindful of the realities of life in the depression, the practical Gwynne signed a pro contract with Smythe of Maple Leaf Gardens in Toronto to fight four matches of four rounds each during the next year with a purse of $250 per fight. His pro career lasted until 1939. In all he had about ninety matches and lost only five. When he lost to Baby Yak by a knockout in 1939, he decided to quit the ring. It was the only time he was ever knocked out.

Lefty Gwynne could never really make a living from boxing. Money was too scarce and despite much newspaper coverage of the sport, the only real drawing power resided with the heavyweights. Thus, al-though a tough and accomplished performer, Gwynne could not get many matches. Boxing, however, was not unkind to him. His reputa-tion as a boxer often helped him obtain work. When Lefty returned to Toronto in triumph after the Olympics he was honoured with a civic reception and a gold watch. After receiving the watch, the ever-practical Gwynne asked the mayor for a job!

1936 Singles Canoeing Francis Amyot Paddling to Gold

Of all the Olympics, the one with the most political overtones, and the one whose politics were most long-lasting was the 1936 Olympiad in Berlin; the so-called "Nazi Olympics".

In 1932, after failing to win more than a few gold medals, the Germans condemned the Olympics as a Jewish international enterprise. Only two years later Hitler used the Berlin Games as a mass rallying focus for the German people, and as a showcase to the world of German physical, technical and moral superiority. No expense was spared despite the fact that Germany suffered as much from the depression as any country in the world. It was to be the biggest, most lavish of all the Olympics and, above all, it was to exceed the effort of the Americans in 1932.

Many technical innovations were introduced: improved photography of the finish line, better loudspeakers, electrical touch recording of strikes in fencing, synchronization of the starter's pistol with the timer's watch, and telephone communication between start and finish lines. The gymnasts were even able to see films of the day's gymnastic events in order to study them for errors and to familiarize themselves with the judging standards.

The improvements were not all technical as far as Germany was concerned. In spite of their poor showing in the Los Angeles Olympics of 1932, the Germans predicted they would win the 1936 Olympics, and they did!

Into this smiling, banner-waving political maelstrom came Francis Amyot of Ottawa who, doubling as a competitor and manager-captain of the canoe team, won Canada's only gold medal.

One of his biggest obstacles was the fact that he could not train in the same type of craft in which he would race. Fortunately, he knew this ahead of time and resourceful as he was, obtained a blueprint of the official canoe to familiarize himself with its dimensions. This canoe was an incredible 45 pounds heavier than the one in which he practised! Had he not been prepared for the disparity between his training and racing canoes, he might easily have been defeated by surprise alone.

But Francis Amyot was not easily defeated by anything. At 31, he was one of Canada's oldest gold medal winners. Blond, well-proportioned, tall and a leader, he was described publicly as, "an outstanding athlete, a most gracious winner, and above all, a gentleman".

He was also the archetypal hero. In 1933 he made a dramatic rescue of three victims of a boating accident. Three football players from the Ottawa Rough Riders had been thrown into the water of Lake Deschenes when their canoe overturned. They were in danger of being swept over the falls when Amyot, paddling furiously, reached them. They clung to the side of his canoe while Amyot battled the current. He managed to hold on until help arrived and the men were pulled to safety.

Amyot's path to the Olympics was a long and arduous one, and it seemed for a long time that he would not make it. He had won the senior Dominion title six times and had been canoeing for thirteen

Seconds after his gold medal win, Francis Amyot, crowned in the then traditional laurel leaves, is carried aloft by his teammates.

105

Charters and Saker	*Williamson*	*Amyot*

years. Canoeing was not on the program of Olympic events before 1936, so it was only natural that such a consistent winner as Francis Amyot should aspire to get there when it was included. Fate, in the form of the Olympic Committee, decided that it would not be easy.

The Olympic funds were short because of the depression. A sports editorial of the day condemned the Canadian Olympic Association. "No credit for Amyot's victory should go to Mulqueen and his group. Not one dime of the $10 000 entrusted to the Olympic committee by the government went to pay the expenses of Frank Amyot." As in many times past, the Olympic Association "bet on the wrong horse", despite Amyot's tremendous record.

These photographs of the Canadian canoeing team were taken during their on-site training sessions at the Olympic rowing course in Grunau, Germany. Harvey Charters and Warren Saker went on to win a silver medal in the 10 000 m doubles and a bronze in the 1000 m doubles.

How then did Francis Amyot get to Berlin? Chief among his fund raisers was his boss in the Department of the Army and Navy Veterans. Captain Gilman saw that Amyot's salary was paid in advance while he was away. In addition he collected donations to the amount of $250 and gave Frank time off for training. The Britannia Canoe Club where Amyot

trained donated $235, the Canadian Canoe Association another $100 and friends contributed $350.

The site of the 2000 m Olympic rowing and canoeing course was at Grunau. A swimming pier 390 feet long had been built into the river to enable twenty canoes to start simultaneously. Elaborate stands capable of seating 30 000 spectators had been built. As it developed, even more thronged into the area for canoeing was a passion with the central Europeans even though the craft originated in North America. Amyot and his seven teammates viewed the site with pleasure. It had obviously been built with foresight. They set to work immediately to get out the kinks brought on by their long voyage.

Francis and his teammates managed to borrow the European canoes and trained diligently. Apart from Amyot, the doubles team of Harvey Charters and Warren Saker of Balmy Beach Canoe Club was held to have the best chance in the nine-event program, and as the pageant unrolled, this prediction held true.

There were 158 competitors from 19 different countries entered in the canoeing events. Amyot was entered in the 1000 m sprint race in which the favourite was Bohuslav Karlik of Czechoslovakia.

Weather conditions were good on the day of the race, and as Amyot prepared to step from the pier to his craft, his teammates solemnly wished him good luck. He lowered himself into his canoe and looked up the course. Ahead, he could see the fluttering of flags that marked the finish line. Around him was the grim silence of the competitors. The canoe moved

Public Archives of Canada

lightly in the water, steadied only at its stern. Francis set his jaw and narrowed his eyes. The starter began his instructions. The time had come.

As the gun sounded, Amyot shot away from the pack with surprising speed. His team thought it might be too fast a pace for him to sustain. Yet, at 500 m he was still in front, his shoulders rippling with the effort. He had become familiar with the heavy canoe in a relatively short time, and had quickly adapted his stroke to the unfamiliar weight. His many years of experience and dogged work were providing him with an advantage. Amyot passed the 700 m mark still in front, but with the favourite, Karlik, closing fast.

As he stroked smoothly toward the brightly coloured flags at the finish line, Francis saw from the corner of his eye the arrow point of Karlik's canoe pushing forward beside him. At each thrust of the paddle, the point came further into Amyot's field of vision and moved inexorably forward until Karlik had taken the lead!

Knowing full well that it had cost Karlik greatly to catch him, Amyot continued his smooth, and flowing paddle stroke. To falter now simply because he had been passed would be the characteristic move of a neophyte. The veteran, the leader, the imperturbable Amyot, could never make such an error. Instead, with no sign of effort, he increased his pace slightly, almost as though he were changing into yet a higher gear as a cyclist might. With 100 m to go, Amyot's canoe began nibbling at the distance separating him from Karlik. The Czech, seeing the challenge, fell into the trap of paddling furiously. His stroke became choppy, and his rhythm uneven. Amyot passed him, bursting into the lead at 50 m. Propelled by the great piston strokes of his arms, Amyot's canoe shot over the finish line in 5:32.1. It was Canada's only gold medal of the 1936 Games!

Francis' team rushed to the dock, hoisted him on to their shoulders and paraded him in front of the grandstand before the cheering thousands. Amyot's moment of glory was enhanced when later Charters and Saker took a silver medal in the 10 000 m race and a bronze in the 1000 m.

When news of Amyot's victory flashed around the world, telegrams of congratulations began to flood in. Two in particular were important. One came from the Prime Minister of Canada, Mr. MacKenzie King, and another from the

Mayor of Ottawa, Mr. Lewis, who immediately began arranging a banquet and reception for this native son.

The banquet was arranged at the Chateau Laurier and there were two hundred and fifty people in attendance. The Honourable C. Power, Minister of Pensions and National Health officially represented the Government of Canada. Power, who had been a member of Ottawa's Silver Seven hockey team, suggested, prophetically enough, that a federal ministry of sport be established to prevent such embarrassment to the Olympic committee as had occurred in Amyot's case. The speeches were many, and the songs and acclaims were all sincere. Finally, as Francis Amyot gave his oak sapling to the mayor (each Olympic gold medallist received a small oak tree) for planting in the city, the mayor in turn gave to him a check for $1000. The money had been raised by subscription from citizens in appreciation of the honour he had brought to the city. Amyot's speech of acceptance was a model of diplomacy:

"In accepting this gift, I cannot help but feel that I am going against the principle of the sport I represented. Paddling is practically the only amateur unit in sport today. But I do appreciate the sentiment behind the gift, and I accept it in that spirit."

The saga of Francis Amyot ended as it began — sincere, unassuming, proud and untouched by the bitterness and wrangling of the rest of mankind.

POST
WORLD
WAR
II

The post World War II period saw vast changes in the Olympics from many standpoints, especially financial. Not only were more funds spent on Olympic facilities, more were spent in preparing athletes for Olympic competitions. This resulted in vast sums being devoted to the training of coaches, sophisticated sports research, coaching aids such as films, TV and radio-telemetry and the construction of new and better facilities everywhere. Not the least cause for this increased interest in the Olympics was the growing realization that the Games offered a forum for the display of political ideologies.

Athletes have benefitted in some ways from governments' political use of the Games. If a government feels strongly that the Olympics are a world stage, it is a matter of national pride, of ideological pride, that its athletes do well. Thus, great care is taken in finding, grooming and preparing the country's best for the world competition. As Olympic fever grows, the unwritten rule becomes "spare no expense".

Since the competition is so fierce, records continue to fall. In 1954, for example, one track expert predicted the "ultimate" performances in track and field. He stated no one would ever break 9.2 s in the 100 yard dash or the mile time of 3:57.8. No one would ever put the shot more than 62 feet, throw the discus more than 200, jump higher than 7 feet, 1 inch, long jump further than 27 feet or pole vault higher than 16. In a dozen years all those marks were broken. Most have subsequently been broken again.

Canada's place in the struggle for political and athletic supremacy has not been high. It is probably a cultural matter rather than a lack of talent. Many countries of equal or smaller populations, such as Hungary, Australia and Cuba, do much better in the medal count because athletics are important in their cultures. One might ask why we don't do as well, relatively speaking, as our US neighbours since our lifestyle is very similar. The answer is that outside of a few professional sports such as hockey, athletics is not an important part of the Canadian way of life. The general attitude of Canadians, government and lay people alike, is an easy tolerance of the presence of sport; "let them run around and have a little fun". This outlook does have its merits but it is no longer sufficient for entering the Olympics.

No matter what the political atmosphere of a country, if it feels the international theatre of sport is important, it will devote a great deal of time and money to the serious training of hundreds, even thousands, of athletes so a few will return home with those cherished discs of metal. Some notable exceptions to this mode have had great success. Kenya's remarkable team of runners all won medals in the 1968 Olympics. Although they were the only athletes entered from that country, they proved the argument that money and effort poured into serious training over a long period of time are necessary to produce winners. In addition to being subsidized, even the team's foreign coach had been brought to the

The stadium complex of the
1976 Montreal Games – the
Olympics 2700 years later.

country and paid by the Kenyan government.

On the other hand, the Canadian government has lagged behind in this course of action and Canadian athletes, for the most part, have lagged behind also. While standards, times and distances have improved in Canada, they have not improved as quickly as everywhere else in the world. Many Canadian athletes have broken old Olympic records in practice or national competition only to find when they face other nations in the Olympics, the other nations have eclipsed the old marks by even greater margins!

Our victories have been in rowing, shooting and horsemanship in the post-war period. In each case the victories were on a highly individual level as the following stories will indicate. The athletes involved achieved their heights on the basis of great personal initiative, resourcefulness, skill and determination. There was virtually no government help behind them.

They worked full time, sandwiching practice sessions between their jobs and sleep; no cushy commission in the Armed Forces so they could practice six hours a day; no payment of wages for lost time from work to attend competitions and no special government grants for equipment, facilities, coaching or anything else. These athletes did it all on their own and can be justifiably proud of their accomplishments.

But the fact remains that there are very few of them.

Canada cannot consider entering the intense competition of the Olympics with any prospects of winning unless a force like Sport Canada continues and expands its operation to put our athletes on a level with those of other, sports-conscious countries. Baron de Coubertin's philosophy aside, the striving for excellence in athletics has become so time-consuming that virtually any athlete must be subsidized in order to reach the top. The extent of Canada's subsidization has been woefully small. Until a few years ago, there was none at all.

With increasing interest in the 1976 Olympics, the amount granted to athletics by the Federal Government has grown each year until it has reached a total of $22 million. It may have been early enough to have an impact on Canada's results in the 76 Games. It may not have an effect until 1980. But there can be no denying that it has already had a positive effect on some performances.

In 1974, Canada won a bronze medal in the world wrestling championships; the first international medal in wrestling for Canada since 1936. The wrestler, Gord Bertie, was a subsidized, albeit modestly, athlete. He received $1800 each year while a student and as a "carded athlete" after graduation, received expense money to attend several international meets every year. His story is typical of the creeping improvement throughout the ranks of Canada's Olympic hopefuls. But only the Olympic competition itself is sufficient to measure just how much improvement has been made.

1952 Trapshooting George Genereux An Olympic Champion at 17

George Genereux was finding it difficult to concentrate on the algebra lesson. It wasn't that he didn't like school – he did. In fact he had already made up his mind to be a doctor and knew he would have to work hard to graduate. He was just finding it hard to get started. People had been extremely nice to him, but distracting; just when he thought the gold medal was put into the background, another award would come along and the whole fuss would start all over again. It was nice but who would think it would go on for so long?

Now his concentration was totally lost. The eighteen-year-old found himself thinking back to when he was a boy of ten accompanying his father to hunt prairie chickens. On the days the two of them went off together, walking, talking and shooting, young George couldn't be happier. A smile flashed across his face as he recalled his first attempts at trapshooting with his father and the dumbfounded looks on everybody's faces as he had smashed clay bird after clay bird.

People called him "a natural", but George still needed all the instruction Jimmy Girgulius could give him. Jimmy was a championship shot himself and he passed on all the little things he had picked up in his years of experience. After a year of Jimmy's instructions, the adults around George decided to send him to Winnipeg to try his hand in the Midwest International. They thought it would be good experience for the thirteen-year-old George to go into competition with marksmen from Manitoba, Saskatchewan, Ontario, Minnesota and the Dakotas. And no one was more surprised than George when he actually won the competition.

From then on George couldn't keep the titles away. He won the Manitoba-Saskatchewan Junior Championship four years in a row, a Class A Championship at Prince Albert in June, 1951, and the Junior title at a Grand Forks, North Dakota Meet in August.

Later in 1951, George decided to enter the biggest of North American meets, the Grand American at

Vandalia, Ohio. He was sixteen years old and went down to the trapshooting centre of North America as a comparative unknown. He came back known by all.

First he won the Junior Championship with 193 out of 200. Then he won the preliminary handicap with 99 out of 100. In the class championship he missed one bird for a score of 199 that tied him with three others. He lost that shoot-off, but won another which gave him the North American Junior championship.

When George got back to Saskatchewan everyone was talking Olympics except him. He knew he had done well in junior competition, but the Olympics would match him with the best in the world. Before coming to a final decision, George entered the Saskatchewan senior championship. When he won that, his selection to the Olympic team was almost automatic.

In preparation for the Olympics, George entered the World Championships in Oslo. It was good training experience because North Americans didn't shoot under World and Olympic championship regulations. In North America, one launching point was used for all the birds. Three different trajectories were possible but they all started from the same point. In the World and Olympic competitions there were three traps and the bird could come from any one of them. But George adapted to the new style quickly. A lot of people were surprised when the news came out of Oslo that a seventeen-year-old displayed nerves of steel in a

Courtesy Nutana Collegiate Institute

115

shoot-off with Sweden's Knut Holmquist to place second in the World
Championship.

Before the Olympics, a reporter
asked George to predict the winning
score. George answered 192 out of
200. Trapshooting is a nerve-
wracking sport; the wind can play
funny tricks and cause the birds to
dip or rise and with only eight
rounds of twenty-five targets each,
competitors couldn't afford to miss
more than one each set and still
win, especially in Olympic class
championships. George didn't know
if it was this reasoning that gave
him the answer or just good luck,
but 192 was the winning score; he
shot it – an Olympic Champion at
seventeen!

George was glad his mother had
come to watch the competition; it
was comfortable knowing that someone close was pulling for him.

In the first day's competition he
had started out well but wasn't
happy with his finish. In the first
three sets of twenty-five he had
only missed one each but in the last
he had missed two giving him a
score of 95. He had to finish
stronger in the next day's shoot and
he knew he could do it. He had shot
higher scores before.

In the first two rounds of the next
day, he scored 24 out of 25 both
times. In the third round he scored
a perfect 25! The last round would
decide; he had to increase his
concentration. He shot the first
twenty-three in a row and missed
the twenty-fourth. He had one last
chance.

Using all his powers of concentration and all his years of experience

George homed in on the 70 mile per hour disc, pulled the trigger and pumped instinctively for the second shot. He didn't need it.

By missing only one in the last round his total score was 192 out of 200 – the score he predicted – but not a winning one yet. Holmquist of Sweden could still tie him if he hit all the birds in his final round.

He hit his first five, ten, twenty, twenty-one fell, twenty-two, twenty-three . . . he missed twenty-four! George Genereux had won a gold medal – the first Canadian to win one since 1936 and the only one of the 1952 Games.

George was surrounded by reporters. It was nice to talk to them, but George was sure the one from the *Toronto Daily Star* thought he was crazy. The reporter came all the way over from the stadium events to interview him, and all

George gets a kiss from mom after winning his Olympic gold medal.

George could do was to ask whether the reporter thought the Detroit Red Wings would stop Gordie Howe from playing baseball!

George was surrounded again, and embarrassed, when some Finnish girls connected with the Games saw him with his medal on and gave him a beautiful bouquet of red roses and a farewell kiss.

When he returned home he found he started to receive a different type of award. First the Canadian Press chose him second to Maurice Richard as their top athlete of 1952. Then people in Toronto contacted him to tell him he had won the Lou Marsh Trophy as Canada's Outstanding Athlete of the Year. George couldn't believe

he had been ranked ahead of athletes like Gordie Howe, Max Bentley, Cliff Lumsden and Ulysses Curtis.

He would have liked to have gone to Toronto to receive the trophy but Canada's only 1952 gold medallist got the mumps. He wasn't going anywhere! So the *Toronto Daily Star* decided to send the trophy to Saskatoon where it could be presented to George at the B'nai B'rith Lodge's "Citizen of the Year" award banquet.

George had plenty of time to prepare himself for the trophy. The news had been announced in January and the presentation was being made in April. He didn't feel the least bit nervous when he accepted the award. Afterwards he sat back hoping to relax through the rest of the evening. Then the spokesman for the panel of judges made the main announcement:

"Ladies and Gentlemen, for his achievements in bringing honour and recognition to the City of Saskatoon, the Citizen of the Year for 1952 is George Genereux."

George's concentration turned abruptly back to the classroom as he heard his teacher call his name. He struggled to recall what the lesson was about. With relief he discovered a photographer was at the door. He wanted to take a photograph of George, away from his guns and trophies, in the halls of his high school. After the photograph was taken, Canada's Outstanding Athlete of the Year, and Olympic Gold Medallist, returned to the classroom to continue his struggle with algebra.

1956 Small-Bore Rifle (Prone) Gerald Ouellette Mr. Bull's-Eye

In 1956 the Olympic Games were held in Australia and the world's problems made their appearance there as well. Egypt, Lebanon and Iraq withdrew from the Games over the Suez incident. Spain, the Netherlands and Switzerland refused to enter because of the Russian invasion of Hungary. The People's Republic of China walked out when the Nationalist Chinese flag was raised at the Olympic Village. Avery Brundage was quoted as saying "In ancient days, nations stopped wars to compete in the Games. Nowadays, we stop the Olympics to continue our wars."

For Canadians, a different type of rifle power made the headlines in December of 1956. For the second consecutive Olympics, a Canadian won a gold medal in shooting. In 1952 it was George Genereux with a shotgun. In 1956 it was Gerry Ouellette with a rifle.

Gerry Ouellette was twenty-two years old when he won his gold medal at Australia. From Windsor, Ontario, he attended Lowe Vocational School where, as a member of the Cadet Corps, he was instructed by Major Wyn. Jennings. From his earliest shooting days, Jennings could see that the youngster had amazing vision, quick reflexes and sound judgment. By 1951 Ouellette had won his first award, finishing in front of three hundred other competitors at an open junior competition in Ottawa. In 1952 he won the Lieutenant-Governor's medal in the open military big-bore class. In that competition he shot fourteen of fifteen bull's-eyes, missing the last one because of nervousness and inexperience. "Marksman" and "Sharpshooter" trophies were among the more than four hundred medals and awards that Ouellette had won

prior to his Olympic victory.

The year 1956 was a busy one for Gerry Ouellette. In addition to his work at the Windsor Ford plant as a tool designer, he was also a corporal in the Canadian Reserve Army, and entered as many rifle competitions as he could. In January there were the Motor City Championships at Dearborn and the Michigan State Tournament at Waterford. In February he entered the South West Michigan Gallery Championship, the Ford Gun Club Hundred Shot Standing Tournament and the Ohio State Championship. After the Canadian and American Rifle Championships he was chosen for the Commonwealth meet at Bisley where he won a first, second and three fourths in spite of a driving rain.

His training program included many hours of skating to develop strong back and leg muscles. Rus-

sian marksmen skated to develop the heavy musculature necessary for a firm stand when firing a 17-pound rifle. He also hunted squirrels; the small, fast-moving animals were hard to hit and kept his reflexes alert. The rest of his time was spent in practice, practice, and practice!

The Olympic trials were scheduled for August in South March, Ontario. It was rumoured there might not be enough money to take two small-bore riflemen to Australia. With Toronto engineer, Gil Boa, one of the favourites, Ouellette knew he had his work cut out. Boa had scored 598 out of 600 in 1954 to win the World's Championship at Venezuela. Ouellette had beaten Boa in the Canadian closed small-bore in 1955, but Boa had won his title back this year.

When the trial results were in, Gerry Ouellette had won his place on the Olympic team by the narrowest of margins over Gil Boa. He joined two trapshooters and a pistol marksman. Fortunately, funds were found to send an additional rifleman, and Gil Boa was selected.

Ouellette looked forward to the competition at the Olympics. The City of Windsor hosted a civic luncheon for its Olympic competitors: Ernestine Russell and Ed Gagnier of the Canadian Gymnastics team and Gerry Ouellette. Prior to leaving for Australia, Ouellette told reporters he wasn't nervous at all. He was looking forward to renewing acquaintances under the Olympic Games conditions since "shooting is personal friendly rivalry at its best".

There was no question that at the 1956 Olympic Games Gerry Ouellette was at his best. In fact he was perfect!

Ouellette had fared poorly in the three-positional rifle shooting competition. The two-man team decided that Boa's rifle was the best one available and they would have a better chance of winning if both used it. But this decision created problems. Each contestant was allowed sixty shots in a two-and-one-half-hour period. Therefore, while they would have to shoot at the same number of targets as everyone else, they would each have half the time!

Boa would go first. Ouellette would keep him posted as to wind changes and the position of the shots on the targets. The confident, thirty-two-year-old Boa had narrowly missed a bronze medal at the 1952 Games, tying for the third spot but slipping back to fourth when it was discovered that his opponent had more bull's-eyes. Now his determination and ability gave him a score of 598 out of 600, the same score he shot in Caracas when he set the world's record. It was Ouellette's turn with just over one hour and fifteen minutes remaining.

The Russian Vasiliy Borisov, a world champion himself, was also entered in the Olympic event and would provide the main competition for the Canadians. Ouellette settled into the prone position at the Williamstown course outside of Melbourne. With the target 50 m away and Gil Boa whispering ad-vice, encouragement, and keeping an eye on the clock, the Windsor native started firing his borrowed gun.

Shot after shot resulted in bull's-eye after bull's-eye. After 40 successive shots dead centre, Ouellette and Boa realized that there was a good chance of winning it all. Boa decided that a break was in order. Ouellette's concentration had been uninterrupted for almost forty-five minutes. He needed a diversion to refresh himself. Some of his shots were beginning to stray to the outer edges of the bull's-eye area. Having talked over the situation and prepared himself for twenty-five more minutes of intense concentration, Gerry Ouellette prepared for his final twenty shots.

The first one was the most important. He had to get back into his rhythm. He took a lot of time measuring the first shot, and with the squeeze of the trigger, the shot was on target! His bull's-eyes continued. When towards the end of his run his shots started to stray again, Boa stepped in again with his encouragement. When the last shot rang out from the borrowed 1952 Winchester Model K and struck the bull's-eye for the sixtieth consecutive time, a triumphant yell went up from the Canadians. Gerry Ouellette had a perfect score of 600.

He needed it. Borisov had scored 599.

Nobody had ever shot a perfect round before. It looked like Ouellette had broken Boa's world record – using Boa's gun to do it! A routine check of the course, however, un-covered a mistake in the distances. In the conversion from yards to metres, course officials were short by a metre and a half. Gil Boa still had his world record and a bronze medal. Gerry Ouellette had his first place and a gold medal. As for the third part of the team, the rifle, it was not an impressive looking specimen. According to Ouellette it was "pretty battered and chips of wood (had) come off at the butt." In its four years of high level international competition, it had won a fourth place at the Helsinki Olympics, a world championship and record at Venezuela in 1954, and a bronze and gold at the 1956 Olympics. "It really belongs to the museum now," said Ouellette.

Both medallists almost fell over themselves in an attempt to thank people. Boa stated "Everybody wants to win but if I couldn't win a gold medal myself, I wanted Gerry to win it. I am delighted with the bronze." Ouellette sent a telegram to the man who started it all back at Lowe Vocational School, Wyn. Jennings.

On his return to Windsor, Gerry Ouellette took up where he left off. Competitions at Bisley, the United States and Moscow found him at or near the top of every meet. He left Windsor to work with the Atomic Energy Commission and later as a high school teacher in Ottawa before returning to Windsor as a drafting teacher at Lowe. In 1967 he was a national winner and a silver medallist at the Pan American Games at Winnipeg.

To Ouellette the pleasure of the sport had come to mean more to

Public Archives of Canada

him than winning medals. Shooting by this time was costing him about two thousand dollars a year. Every other weekend from 1966 to 1968 Gerry Ouellette drove to Kitchener, a return trip of about 300 miles, in order to practise in suitable surroundings. Yet, in spite of all his sacrifices he almost declined the invitation to go to the 1968 Mexico Olympics.

In an effort to ensure that they could perform at the high altitude, the Olympic Committee asked all athletes to fill in various forms and charts. Ouellette objected, saying he couldn't see the relevance for a marksman. "When I got all those forms and charts I told them to please let me know if I had to go through that to go to Mexico. I said if I had to, they didn't have to bother taking me," he explained with a chuckle. Ouellette was sixth in 1968, barely missing a medal in his first visit back to the Olympic Games, twelve years after his perfect score.

1956
Coxswainless Fours Arnold, d'Hondt, Loomer & McKinnon
The Cinderella Four

There are many tales in the annals of the Olympics which tell of athletes reaching unparalleled heights and then falling back to more ordinary levels; others have won in a completely unexpected fashion, and still others who were "sure bets" gave disappointing performances. Most unusual of all is, perhaps, the Cinderella team. For one individual to outperform his past record is surprising enough, but for a group to do it is almost impossible. However, it was such a group, the four-oared shell without coxswain, which won a gold medal for Canada in the 1956 Olympics.

The team came together almost by accident. All four were freshmen at the University of British Columbia in the fall of 1955. Only one, Don Arnold, had rowed before, and he had only one year of experience. The others, Archie McKinnon, Walt d'Hondt and Lorne Loomer, had never seen a racing shell until that year. All four came from small towns in the interior of British

Columbia.

Under the watchful eye of the great BC coach, Frank Read, the four were among many other hopefuls who began training in February, 1956 in big, thirty-two-man barges on the chilly waters of Coal Harbour, Vancouver. They all hoped to make the heavy eight or, failing that, the four-oared crew.

The eight was well-established because it had won a gold medal in the 1954 British Empire Games, and had placed second in the 1955 World Henley Regatta. Coach Read did not want to tamper too much with a winner. The four, however, was up for grabs and, after some months of spring training, d'Hondt, Loomer, McKinnon and Hughes (stroke) made up the crew. Don Arnold was selected as a spare for either crew.

When classes at UBC had ended, the crew decided that the only effective way of training together was to live together. The house they agreed to rent would certainly never feature in *Better Homes and Gardens*. There wasn't a stick of furniture in the place, and not a single pane of glass in the windows. UBC donated some bunk beds for the athletes, and meals were taken at the Vancouver Boat Club. The summer adventure was underway.

Not, however, without difficulties. Although they had spirit to spare, the crew had no money, and spirit has never yet paid a bill. Each rower worked as a labourer, but financial support had to be arranged to buy equipment — a shell costs about $3000 and oars about $50 each.

Because of the pounding a shell takes in ocean practice, a training shell could never be used in an actual race. The shell in which the crew won the Canadian championship was used afterwards to train for the Olympics. It received forty-two patches and two splits between July and October.

Then into the picture came the Lieutenant-Governor of British Columbia, Frank Ross, and his business partner, Colonel Victor Spencer. These two gentlemen appointed a business manager, Nellis Stacey, to look into the crew's financial problems, including the purchase of equipment. Another businessman, Jack Diamond, contributed all the meat the crew needed, while other businesses donated a freezer and kitchen utensils. With the whole community behind them, the steady grind of practice became a little easier to accept.

Now came the mind-numbing, muscle-racking routine. Every day of the week the crew arose at 4:15 and met with Read at 5:00 on the water. After a 15 mile row they returned to breakfast and then dispersed to their various jobs. Every evening at 5:00 they were back on the water with Read for a 20 mile row and by 9:00 were in bed. On weekends, for variety, the crew rowed 30 miles each day. One can only look at that routine and be awed. Where could one gather a group of people willing to practise four hours a day, seven days a week, and still keep a full-time job?

A special approach had to be taken by Read to the four-oared crew. He knew the great potential of the eight-oared crew and would do nothing to risk its chances. The four was put together solely for the purpose of providing training for the spares in the eight-oared crew. Therefore it took second priority in everything. Coach Read was forced to lay down certain rules so that both crews could benefit from his coaching. Thus the four's, to capitalize on Coach Read's time, had to row fast enough to keep even with the eight-oared shell. Regardless of water conditions, the four-oared crew could be no more than thirty seconds behind the big crew in the daily time trials. This made rowing extremely demanding on the athletes in the smaller boat.

At this point in the summer came two disruptions of the well-laid plans. The public health authorities condemned the crew's house as unfit for human habitation, and Hughes, the stroke, left the crew to go to Germany. The first problem was easily solved: the oarsmen simply moved into the dancehall of the Vancouver Boat Club and continued their spartan lives. The second problem was temporarily solved when Don Arnold, a farm boy from Rutland, moved into the stroke seat vacated by Hughes. But simply adding a body to three others doesn't make a crew.

On their first morning in Coal Harbour's grey waters, the loss of balance, rhythm and timing brought about by the change in the stroke seat caused the shell to tip. Nothing would go right. The crew fought among themselves. Salt water soaked them; their thighs bled from the constant scraping of their thumbnails because of the uneven stroke and loss of balance. Finally they returned to shore and stumbled into breakfast confused, demoralized, soaked and bleeding. The Olympics seemed a ridiculous dream for four freshmen rowing together for the first time with trials a scant six weeks away.

Adversity, fortunately, often makes strong individuals become stronger. This seemed to be the case with Arnold, d'Hondt, Loomer and McKinnon. They fought and cursed, but never considered quitting. They discussed the problems nightly and hoped for solutions daily. They shifted one another to different seats to try for better

Archie McKinnon, Lorne Loomer, Walter d'Hondt and Don Arnold Before a race . . .

balance (Once, with short-sighted Lorne Loomer in the bow, they rammed an American submarine half-submerged in the harbour!), and they made up in endurance

. . . and after.

and strength what they lacked in balance and timing. Soon they were able to stay with the eights during the daily time trials.

Both crews won easily at the Canadian Henley in St. Catharines, and both set records. The four-

oared shell with Arnold stroking finished the 2000 m course in its customary thrashing style in 6:05.8, beating the Olympic record by 20 s! And they hadn't yet reached their peak! They clawed and grabbed their way down the course cursing

126

and fighting every watery inch, bound and determined to finish first – and only then did they check to see if they had looked good doing it. They hadn't.

Perhaps their awkward appearance was what influenced the decision of the Canadian Rowing Association. At a party after the finals, it was announced that only the eight-oared crew would be sent to the Olympics.

The hopes of the four were dashed. How could the Association overlook their record time – never mind how they looked? Once again Frank Ross and Colonel Spencer came to the rescue. They announced to the Canadian Olympic Association that they would personally fund the transportation of the four to Australia if the Olympic Association did not feel they were worth risking the money on.

The Olympics were to be held in October – spring in Australia – so the four-oared crew had two months to polish their style.

The pace intensified. Training runs of 30 miles became commonplace. Films of their practices were studied by the crew so they could correct minor individual flaws and improve timing and rhythm. The morning workouts were abandoned in favour of a 5:00 run around Stanley Park – a distance of 11 miles. Meets were arranged with the Universities of Seattle and Washington. After their last practice run before leaving for Australia, the fours were still not sure they were at their peak. Some rough spots still remained.

Meanwhile, in Australia, Olympic preparations were pulling out of their initial shambles. (Avery Brundage, chairman of the International Olympic Committee, had gone to Australia at one point and threatened to withdraw the Games if preparations were not speeded up. As it was, the equestrian events were held in Stockholm, Sweden.) The rowing course at Lake Wendouree near Melbourne, had been well prepared. It was in the centre of the long, 5 foot deep lake, flanked on each side by giant beds of water weeds, grown specifically to ensure calm water.

In their first heat, Arnold, Loomer, d'Hondt and McKinnon set out to better the Olympic record. Their normal race strategy had been to go very hard for the first 500 m, settle into a nice, steady pace for the next 1000, and finally go hard with everything they had for the last 500. (Today this might be called progressive anaerobic training.)

The four had a tactic they called a "Big Ten". This meant ten of the hardest, fastest strokes they could put together no matter where they were in a race. Thus, if challenged for the lead by another boat, Arnold would call for a "Big Ten" to beat off the challenge.

In their first heat, the four hit their sweep oars hard and stroked the course unchallenged to finish in 6:36.6 – just 0.6 s off the Olympic record. They had not duplicated the fine finish they achieved at the Canadian Henley, but they had finished well ahead of the pack.

In the second heat, they coasted home, saving everything for the final heat against their biggest rival, the USA. In the final race they decided, once again, to go for the record, despite a rather stiff head wind which had increased steadily over the four days of competition. Tension made them edgy and snappish with each other. They hunched over their sweeps waiting for the dropping of the starter's flag. This was the high point, the final: the gold medal and all they had worked for was on the line. At the sound of the starter's "Partez!" they all pulled together; to a man, they virtually missed the water, throwing four blades of spray at their boat holder. The rest of the field went off like jack rabbits.

Arnold had two choices. He could tell them to get out of the boat and walk home, or he could call for an easy power stroke to settle them and ride out the panic. He chose the latter, and they swung into the course far in the wake of the others. When he felt them smooth out, Arnold called for their normal heavy stroke for 500 m. The boat surged ahead like an arrow as the four reached down in those deep reserves that marked them for gold.

Then Arnold hoarsely called for a "Big Ten" and they powered past the last boat in line. At the 500 m mark they caught two more of their opponents. At 800 m, only the Americans were in front of them, and at the half-way point Arnold called for another "Big Ten". Hundreds of miles and hundreds of hours of training, denial and sacrifice gave them the ten strokes – ten powerful, driving strokes – that pushed them out in front to stay.

They hit the finish line five full boat lengths ahead of second place in a time of 7:08.8. They had won an Olympic gold medal – Canada's first gold medal in rowing.

The saga of the Cinderella four did not end with their Olympic victory. They progressed to the eight-oared shell which won the British Empire Games gold medal in 1958. Then they decided to retire. With the Rome Olympics of 1960 on the horizon, the athletic director of UBC, Mr. Phillips, persuaded them to go back into training with the heavy eight. This time the training grind and the sacrifices seemed harder. Frank Read, their coach, was a little older, and a little more tired. They stuck it out, however, and finished their careers in the eight-oared crew which won the silver medal in the 1960 Olympics.

The four freshmen from land-locked towns in BC had woven a saga in Canadian sports history whose example of stamina, courage and dedication is unmatched.

The medal presentation at Melbourne.

1964
Coxswainless Pairs Hungerford & Jackson The Pair That Shouldn't Be

Roger Jackson and George Hungerford rowed at a steady pace to the starting line of the final race in the Olympic 2000 m competition for paired oars without coxswain. On the Toda rowing course proper, just to their left, the final race of the fours with coxswain was sweeping down to the finish line. Jackson and Hungerford looked at the race distractedly. They were concentrating on what they would do in their own seven-minute moment on the Olympic stage. In their wake they could see the vaunted German crew and further back the smaller but smoother-stroking pair from Holland. Their greatest challenge would come from these two crews. Jackson and Hungerford were anxious, but not tense. They felt that anyone who could beat them deserved to do so, for they themselves could not have prepared more thoroughly than they already had.

The 1964 Olympics in Tokyo were the first ever held in Asia. They were a marvel of organization and planning. The only major complaint came from the Japanese athletes who tired of a high protein diet of chicken and steak and had a craving for some traditional Japanese food. Even the weather seemed controlled by the Olympics organization. Rain had fallen for days before, but as the opening ceremonies began, the skies cleared and 7169 athletes from 95 countries paraded into the vast stadium before 72 000 spectators. Jet planes looped their coloured exhaust gases into the five interlocking circles of the Olympic symbol and the largest Games ever were underway.

The 1964 Olympic Games saw many Canadian achievements. Jenny Wingerson was the first female standard bearer in the march past, and trackmen Harry Jerome and Bill Crothers won bronze and silver medals respectively to give Canada two track medals for the first time in twenty-five years. The only gold medallists, however, were Roger Jackson and George Hungerford.

The two oarsmen were at the Olympics only after a bizarre series of incidents that included serious illness, crew changes, frustrating Canadian qualifying races and a decision at one point not to go to the Olympics at all! They were also rowing in a borrowed shell, and had only rowed together for six weeks. Their win was such a stunning surprise that no Canadian newspapermen were there at the time. They were all watching Jerome and Crothers in the stadium.

The preparations for the final race for paired oars without coxswain were nearly finished. Six shells pointed straight out from the starting platform, their sterns held by men lying prone on the dock to steady them. The starter began his countdown. To each crew in turn he called out "Êtes-vous prêts? Are you ready?" Jackson and Hungerford thought how very ready they were.

Since May, they had been rowing twice a day in the tradition of the great BC crews. Like other crews, they too, had banded together to rent a house, hire a cook and live rowing. Six months earlier, Jackson

had been a member of a fine four-oared crew and Hungerford a member of the prestigious heavy eight-oared crew of the Vancouver Rowing Club. Their days had consisted of a morning workout from 5:30 to 7:30 a.m. and an afternoon practice from 5:30 to 7:30 p.m. Between these two sessions they worked as labourers.

As the time for the Canadian trials drew near, the crews worked harder. They perfected their co-ordination of stroke; increased their endurance and improved their speed. After each practice they plodded wearily up the long flight of steps from the dock barely able to lift one foot above the other, grasping the handrail for support.

A few days before the trials at the Canadian Henley course on July 21, the bowman in the four-oared shell strained his back and could not row. A spare, picked up from the doubles' crew, was just recovering from a similar ailment

Roger Jackson, in the dark shirt, training with the four-oared crew before being teamed with Hungerford.

and was not an adequate replacement. As a result, the excellent four-oared crew from Vancouver which could actually defeat the vaunted eight-oared shell did not win the trials and was not picked to go to the Olympics while the heavy eight swept to an easy victory and was selected. Coach Glen Mervyn named Roger Jackson and Wayne Pretty from the four-oared crew as alternates to the eight. Jackson received the news coldly. He did not fancy the role of spare and he was especially dejected because he knew his four-oared crew was good enough to win an Olympic medal. He thought he would rather not go to the Olympics under those conditions.

As compensation, the spares for the eight would be entered in the

doubles competition. Jackson set to work with Pretty to make themselves a respectable crew. But in August, George Hungerford in the eight-oared shell was struck down by mononucleosis and Pretty, who rowed on the same side, was moved into Hungerford's seat. Jackson was without a regular partner and the Olympics were in October. By early September Hungerford had recovered sufficiently to resume training as a spare for the eight. Thus he was finally teamed with Jackson.

The pairing turned out to be as close to a perfect match as was ever attained. Hungerford was 6 feet, 4 inches while Jackson was 6 feet, 5 inches; both weighed about 185 pounds, were extremely competitive, and had enormous self-discipline. But the six short weeks to the Olympics were simply not going to be enough time. Everyone knew that a paired crew had to train for years to attain the degree of balance and rhythm

necessary for success. Each had to learn the nuances of the other's actions in order to react quickly and automatically to the changes that were vital to steering, sprinting and pacing. To make matters worse, Hungerford still had mononucleosis and, after their morning practices, had to rest in bed until the afternoon workout. He was noticeably weaker in the second practice of the day.

Still they persisted. In order to get maximum efficiency into their stroke, the oarsmen removed the rudder from the shell. In this manner, they could tell if one man was not pulling as powerfully as the other, for if one pulled less, the stronger man would force the boat to circle. As Hungerford's strength slowly returned, they made sure that their rowing was well-timed and synchronized. They became very proficient at steering and they were able to direct all their limited energy into propelling the shell rather than compensating for improper handling.

In the first workout on the Toda course, the eight-oared shell finished first, of course, but they were so impressed at the powerful, efficient pull of Hungerford and Jackson knifing through the water behind them that they did a very unusual thing. Resting on their oars watching the swiftly approaching pair, the crew of the eight spontaneously broke into applause! It was a good sign for the forthcoming competition.

In the first heat of the paired oars

The gold medal presentation.

race, things went well for Hungerford and Jackson. From the start they held a close third place position until the 1500 m mark and then they decided to move ahead. The inexperienced Finns rowing beside them tried unsuccessfully to keep the same pace. As the Finns dropped behind, they began to veer into the Canadian lane. Jackson in his stroke seat could see the Finns coming closer and closer. He realized that if they were fouled, the Finns would be disqualified, and the race would have to be rerowed. With the realization that Hungerford might not have too many hard races in him due to his illness, Jackson made a quick decision. He did not want the race rerowed, so he pulled the Canadian boat well to one side of their own lane and called for a sprint. Although the official later commended them for their sportsmanlike conduct in avoiding a collision with the Finns, the actual motivation for their move was less altruistic.

The sprint moved them into the lead which they held to the end. They heard the finishing buzzer drone in the fine time of 7:19:78, well ahead of the second place Danes. When they compared their time to that of the great German crew of Schwan and Wottenrot who had managed a 7:20:18, they were very pleased and solemnly shook hands.

The following day, the eight-oared shell from Canada was eliminated from medal contention, so Canada's hopes on the water fell squarely on the shoulders of these two men who by all rights should

not even have been at the Olympics.

On Thursday morning, four days after winning their heat, they prepared for their run at a gold medal. After a breakfast of scrambled eggs, fruit and tea, Jackson and Hungerford polished the delicate skin of their borrowed shell. The shell belonged to the University of Washington; the kindly Americans had loaned them a good shell which had been built eight years previously for two University of Washington oarsmen, Fifer and Hecht, who had competed in the 1956 Olympics and won a gold medal in the same shell!

And now they sat awaiting the final word and the dropping of the flag which was to send them down the course for seven minutes of the most demanding of sports activities. Concentrating as they were, they saw but did not register the starting tower and floats, the lane markers or their boat holder. There was silence, the light slapping of the waves, then "Partez" bellowed from the speaker suspended above them. The flag dropped. They dug viciously at the water; the race had begun.

As in their first race, Jackson and Hungerford began at 43 strokes per minute, dropped the pace somewhat as they surged to a slight lead and then held steady. The first half of a race is a very difficult physical effort, but the last half is much worse. Races are lost when one crew cannot ignore the pleadings of their bodies to stop the punishment while another crew is capable of pushing hard right to the end. Jackson and Hungerford were capable of that sustained effort which

The expressions on their faces could be the result of the fantastic effort they made to win their gold medals or the fact that, to celebrate their victory, they immediately drank seven Colas each.

marked champions.

As they passed the halfway point, Jackson could see the other boats and felt the race was under tenuous but definite control, despite the fact that Hungerford's oar was dipping into the Finn's lane. They had drifted slightly because of the crosswind. To husband their strength, especially that of the recovering Hungerford, Jackson had decided not to sprint, but to maintain a steady rhythm. So far his plan was working. At 1500 m they held a 1.5 boat length lead.

The smooth-stroking Dutch crew suddenly began to pull up. First, they narrowed the lead. Next, their bow was even with the stern of the Canadian shell. Gradually, it crept up even with the midpoint. With barely 100 m to go, Jackson was forced to go into a sprint — something he did not feel they could do.

"Up!" called Jackson in desperation. On the first sprint stroke, the craft shuddered almost like a runner staggering. On the second stroke, the marvellous synchronous rhythm returned and the two boats, Canadian and Dutch, sped down to the finish line in half a dozen quick pulls. They crossed virtually together and two quick "beeps" sounded from the finish horn. But who had been first?

Without waiting to see what names would flash on the scoreboard, Jackson twisted tiredly in his seat to grasp and shake the limp hand of the nearly unconscious Hungerford. The two waited out an agonizing thirty seconds until the last shell finished. Then the results were signalled for all the crowd to see. Jackson and Hungerford had won the gold medal!

After they had rowed back down the course and taken their shell from the water, they celebrated, gold medals around their necks, by drinking seven Cokes each! Sitting in the stands feeling satisfied, they did not know they were the objects of a concerted search by the newsmen who wanted to interview them — the same newsmen who had all gone to the track events instead.

At 9:30, while Hungerford and Jackson prepared for an early night's rest, the newspapermen were combing Tokyo's Ginza strip looking for the two gold medallists out celebrating. One enterprising reporter even phoned Vancouver to ask George Hungerford's father where he thought George might be. An elaborate check-in system, prepared so any reporter who located the Canadian heroes could report their whereabouts to a central telephone number, failed to produce a clue.

Next morning, after a leisurely and large breakfast, Roger Jackson and George Hungerford revelled in the unaccustomed luxury of no practice. As they sauntered towards the gate intent on dismantling and packing their reliable shell, they ran head-on into a phalanx of reporters armed with recorders, and typewriters who had finally run their prey to ground in the least likely of places – the athletes' village.

Although the pair did win the Lou Marsh Trophy as the outstanding athletes in Canada in 1964, their further exploits on the water were obscured by the shine of their Olympic medals. Counting their two Olympic races, they rowed together in competition a total of five times. Hungerford, who gave up rugger for rowing only because of a damaged shoulder, retired in the spring following the Olympics. Jackson placed eleventh in the 1968 Olympics as a sculler and twelfth in the 1972 Olympics as a member of the crew of a fours with coxswain.

Never again did he duplicate the peak of performance he reached in his perfect match with Hungerford.

1968 Equestrian Grand Prix (Jumping) Day, Elder & Gayford The $100 000 Medal

The three riders, splendidly dressed in red tunics, white breeches and black boots made an impressive sight. They were seated high on their mounts and stepping proudly across the infield of the huge Olympic stadium to their destination – the winners' stand where President Gustavo Ordaz Diaz of Mexico, in front of 80 000 spectators, would present them with the last gold medal of the 1968 Olympics.

Obviously delighted, Prince Philip strode smartly towards the three, shook their hands, and chatted animatedly with them while patting their horses. The three dismounted; the President paused in

front of each one and made the medal presentation. The huge crowd was hushed now and the band played "O Canada" as the Maple Leaf made its way to the top of the flag pole. With little encouragement and to everyone's surprise, Jim Day riding Canadian Club, Jim Elder on The Immigrant and Tom Gayford on Big Dee had won a gold medal for Canada in the Grand Prix (Jumping) event of the Equestrian competitions.

Equestrianism can be defined as the art of minimizing obstacles — both on and off the riding course. It has always carried with it an aristocratic notion, identified in many people's minds as a "rich man's sport" and not a demanding one at that.

Canadian equestrian teams have always had problems in being accepted as legitimate Olympic contenders in spite of successes enjoyed since the first Olympic team was formed for the Helsinki Olympics in 1952. Those Games were a series of misfortunes — injuries to horses, sickness, falls — yet Tom Gayford was able to say the effort was worthwhile. He knew that Canada was well qualified to compete in equestrian events, that Canada "given proper support could conceivably win". The 1952 funds were so limited the equestrian team could only return to Canada by wiring home a personal guaran-

Prince Philip walks away from the winners' stand after talking with the victorious Canadian team: Jim Elder, Jim Day and Tom Gayford. ◀

tee to a travel agency.

The 1956 Games bore out Gayford's belief. John Rumble, Jim Elder and Brian Herbinson won a bronze in the three-day equestrian event, finishing a full forty-six points ahead of fourth place Australia.

Following a resounding gold medal win in the 1959 Pan American games, Canada seemed to be a serious contender in the 1960 Olympics at Rome. In a gruelling three-day competition in which it was estimated that sixty per cent of the horses which finished were injured, the Canadian team was eliminated when one of its riders was unable to finish the race. Three years' training and $170 000 were lost as the Canadian team was obliged to drop out, not having a full team.

At the 1964 Games in Tokyo, two women made up Canada's Olympic equestrian team; the other riders simply decided they couldn't afford to go. However, a turning point was reached when sporting and national interests were placed before commercial and personal gains: it was decided to end the "horse drain". Canadian team members had for some years taken great pains to train world class jumping horses. There was a growing demand for them and they represented a profitable and enjoyable way to make a living while training for the growing number of equestrian events they were being invited to. Rather than sell the horses to foreign interests, the owners and team members agreed to retain them and build a strong

team for the 1967 Pan American games and the 1968 Olympics.

Their resolution was put to the test after the Winnipeg Pan Ams. Jim Day, riding Canadian Club, won an individual gold medal. Day was part owner of Canadian Club and had intended to sell him after the Pan American events; but with the success of the horse, he bought out his partner's share and turned down offers from both the American and British teams. "I got a little gold medal fever," he said. "I felt the horse should be available for the Canadian team in the Olympics."

With that type of attitude, the Canadians prepared themselves for the 1968 Mexico Olympics, even though it seemed at times they were all on their own. The Canadian Olympic committee was prepared to pay for the expenses of the team of eleven riders and five officials, but wouldn't or couldn't provide funds for the mounts. It was up to the equestrian team to supply the horses as well as pay for the expenses involved in sending the animals to Mexico. With donations from private individuals as well as large foundation grants and the selling of pins, pictures and postcards, the money was raised.

When the sixteen horses were put into a specially prepared plane there was some concern about their safety. Stalls were arranged three in a row; the two outside horses had insufficient head room, a factor that could craze a horse

Jim Day on Canadian Club.

while in flight causing him to kick at the sides of the plane and incite the other horses. A veterinarian accompanied the animals with orders to destroy any animal in such an emergency. None occurred however, and the members of the equestrian team soon joined the horses in Mexico.

Three men and three horses figured prominently in the gold medal event. The youngest, Jim Day, was a twenty-one-year-old car salesman from King City, Ontario. He had been around horses for much of his life; his parents operated a horse breeding and training school at Thornhill, Ontario. His interest in equestrianism was spurred on by a visit to the Royal Winter Fair and he went on to become North American Junior and Senior Champion. His mount was Canadian Club, a thoroughbred which had proven too difficult to train for the track. Purchased for $500, the horse spent two years at the Day stable before being trained for equestrian events. His temperament was such that he was liable to kick, bite, balk and stumble in practice sessions. In competitions, he was likely to "strut like a Hollywood starlet". It was estimated that Canadian Club was worth about $75 000 in 1968.

The oldest member of the three-man team was Tom Gayford, a thirty-eight-year-old stockbroker. He was a twenty-year veteran of international competition, a member of Canada's equestrian team in 1952 as well as the medal team of the 1959 and 1967 Pan American games. Gayford's mount was

another thoroughbred, Big Dee. It had been in only one major international competition – the 1967 Pan American games at Winnipeg. For a time, Big Dee's status was doubtful. The big brown horse developed a near fatal case of colic six days prior to the competition. As Grand Prix day approached, Big Dee's condition improved. Gayford decided to chance it and stay with the experienced but somewhat weakened horse.

The third member of the team was Jim Elder, a thirty-four-year-old businessman from Aurora. Elder had been riding since he was ten, and honours seemed to follow him. He was International Jumping Champion at the Royal Winter Fair in 1960, 1961 and 1964 as well as a medal winner at the 1959 and 1967 Pan Ams and the 1956 Olympics. Jim Elder's original choice for the competition was to be his reliable Pieces of Eight. The horse, however, developed pleurisy in one lung. Elder switched to The Immigrant, "a rather ornery six-year-old who kicks out his hind legs after each jump". Elder was able to ride the seventeen-hand gelding in the individual Jumping Grand Prix where the pair finished a close sixth.

Fifteen nations had entered at the Estadio Olympico. None were allowed to practice on the course. It was only on the morning of the event that competitors were allowed to walk around the grounds. It was a compact course. The fourteen obstacles with seventeen jumps seemed to be closer together than

Jim Elder on The Immigrant.

140

normal. The brightly painted jumps and obstacles, decorated with abundantly colourful paper flowers and Aztec symbols didn't hide the fact that it was a demanding course.

Each member of the team was required to go through the course twice, each circuit being completed within a time limit of 96 seconds. Each second over the time limit carried a penalty of 0.25 points to a maximum of 120 seconds. Over two minutes meant disqualification. Other penalties included 4 points if the height of an obstacle was in any way lowered, 3 points for balking or refusing to overcome an obstacle (three such refusals resulting in disqualification); and 6 points for a competitor who fell off. At the end of each rider's circuit, the penalty points were totalled for each team. The group having the lowest number of penalty points would win the competition.

The favourites were the teams of West Germany, winners of the previous three Olympic events, Britain, the USA and France. The Canadian team was all but ignored; only a West German magazine chose to mention them as possible "dark horses". In Canada, *The Globe and Mail* predicted a placing in the top three; the *Toronto Star* said the top six, and the Chairman of the Equestrian Team, Dennis Whitaker, indicated he would be pleased with a fifth or sixth for Canada's first-ever Grand Prix team.

Encouraged by a great first round ride by Jim Elder on The Immigrant who was assessed 9.25 penalty faults, the Canadians ended the first half of the competition with 49.5 points, in second place behind Great Britain's 48. Elder's ride was brilliant. Day had accumulated 18 points, Gayford 22.25. As the afternoon round commenced the British were disqualified when their silver medallist in the individual competition, Marion Cookes, was thrown when her horse refused to jump. With the British eliminated, France seemed to be ready to forge ahead until D'Oriola suffered 29.5 penalty points in his second round.

Meanwhile the Canadians had been efficiently making their way through the maze of obstacles. Gayford's second run was cut down to 17.25 points; Day maintained his steadiness with another 18. Only Elder was left. If he could keep his ride under 26 penalty points, the gold would belong to Canada. The crowd loved watching The Immigrant kick out his hind legs after each jump, but the near misses almost turned the Canadian team into nervous wrecks. The Immigrant knocked down four jumps and Elder accumulated a respectable 18-point score, low enough to give the Canadians the gold medal on an accumulated total of 102.75 penalty points. France was second with 116.5, West Germany third with 117.75.

The equestrian team was euphoric, but the event went almost unnoticed in Canada. Most of the media representatives and the Canadian Olympic team's Chef De Mission, Howard Radford, had already left for Canada.

The trip home was almost as demanding as the competition. While Elder and Gayford returned home the next day, October 29th, Jim Day and five grooms were left behind to accompany the $750 000 cargo of sixteen horses in a chartered DC-7. Because of Mexico City's high altitude, it was only partially fuelled up, and was scheduled to land at Brownsville, Texas for refuelling. When American customs officials demanded that the horses be unloaded and sprayed for disease, the plane decided to land at Matamoros, Mexico instead. The fuel that was shipped from across the Texas border to Matamoros turned out to be a lower octane than required; to make matters worse, the truck's fuel pump wouldn't operate. Some hurried adjustments were made to the engines, a hand pump was found and 4000 gallons of fuel were pumped into the plane's tanks.

Shortly after take off an engine gave out, necessitating a forced landing at Houston. After much debate, the US customs officials gave permission to leave the horses on the plane for the fourteen hours needed to fix the engine. Finally, the plane took off and, battling strong headwinds which doubled the flying time, arrived back in Toronto one day later than scheduled.

All told, the team had travelled 9000 miles, spent $100 000, and undergone sickness and physical and mental strain for the one goal that made it all worthwhile – a gold medal.

Tom Gayford on Big Dee.

Canada's Olympic Medallists

1904 St. Louis
Gold	The Winnipeg Shamrocks Lacrosse Club	*Lacrosse*
	Etienne Desmarteau	*56-pound Weight Throw*
	George Seymour Lyon	*Golf*
	The Galt Association Football Club	*Soccer*
Silver	Toronto Argonauts Rowing Team	*Senior Eights*

1906 Athens
Gold	Billy Sherring	*Marathon*
Silver	Donald Linden	*1500 m Walk*

1908 London
Gold	Bobby Kerr	*200 m*
	The All Canadas	*Lacrosse*
	Walter Ewing	*Trapshooting*
Silver	Garfield McDonald	*Triple Jump*
	Cornelius Walsh	*Hammer Throw*
	George Beattie	*Trapshooting*
Bronze	Bobby Kerr	*100 m*
	Ernest Archibald	*Pole Vault*
	Calvin Bricker	*Broad Jump*
	A. Cote	*Bantamweight Wrestling*
	Army Gun Team	*Army Gun-Team Shooting*
	Canadian Cycling Team	*Team Pursuit*
	Coxswainless Pairs	

1912 Stockholm
Gold	George Goulding	*10 000 m Walk*
	George Hodgson	*400 m Swim*
	George Hodgson	*1500 m Swim*
Silver	Calvin Bricker	*Broad Jump*
	Duncan Gillis	*Hammer Throw*
Bronze	William Hapeny	*Pole Vault (tie)*
	Frank Lukeman	*Pentathlon*
	Everett Butler	*Single Sculls*

1920 Antwerp
Gold	Earl Thomson	*110 m Hurdles*
	Albert Schneider	*Welterweight Boxing*
Silver	C. G. Graham	*Bantamweight Boxing*
	Pru d'Homme	*Middleweight Boxing*
	George Vernot	*1500 m Swim*
Bronze	C. Newton	*Lightweight Boxing*
	George Vernot	*400 m Swim*
	M. Herscovitch	*Middleweight Boxing*

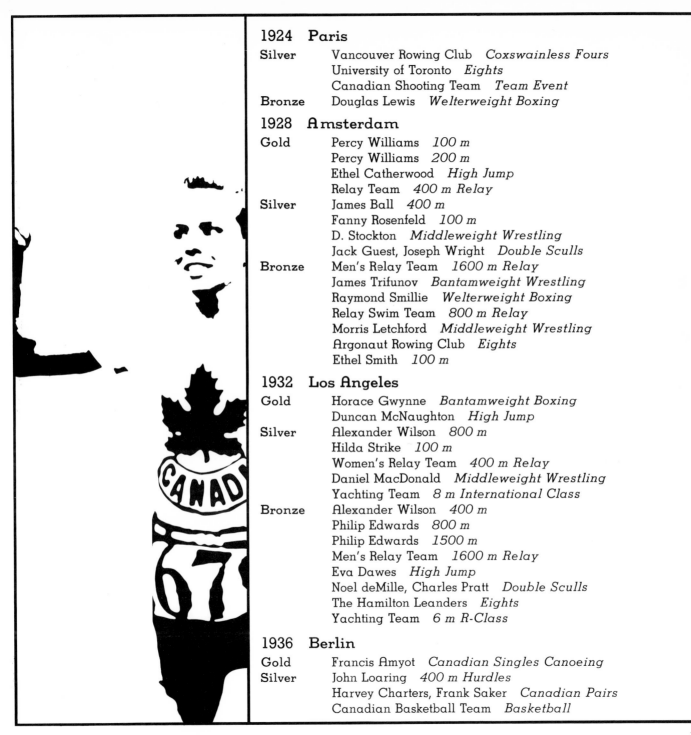

1924 Paris

Silver	Vancouver Rowing Club	*Coxswainless Fours*
	University of Toronto	*Eights*
	Canadian Shooting Team	*Team Event*
Bronze	Douglas Lewis	*Welterweight Boxing*

1928 Amsterdam

Gold	Percy Williams	*100 m*
	Percy Williams	*200 m*
	Ethel Catherwood	*High Jump*
	Relay Team	*400 m Relay*
Silver	James Ball	*400 m*
	Fanny Rosenfeld	*100 m*
	D. Stockton	*Middleweight Wrestling*
	Jack Guest, Joseph Wright	*Double Sculls*
Bronze	Men's Relay Team	*1600 m Relay*
	James Trifunov	*Bantamweight Wrestling*
	Raymond Smillie	*Welterweight Boxing*
	Relay Swim Team	*800 m Relay*
	Morris Letchford	*Middleweight Wrestling*
	Argonaut Rowing Club	*Eights*
	Ethel Smith	*100 m*

1932 Los Angeles

Gold	Horace Gwynne	*Bantamweight Boxing*
	Duncan McNaughton	*High Jump*
Silver	Alexander Wilson	*800 m*
	Hilda Strike	*100 m*
	Women's Relay Team	*400 m Relay*
	Daniel MacDonald	*Middleweight Wrestling*
	Yachting Team	*8 m International Class*
Bronze	Alexander Wilson	*400 m*
	Philip Edwards	*800 m*
	Philip Edwards	*1500 m*
	Men's Relay Team	*1600 m Relay*
	Eva Dawes	*High Jump*
	Noel deMille, Charles Pratt	*Double Sculls*
	The Hamilton Leanders	*Eights*
	Yachting Team	*6 m R-Class*

1936 Berlin

Gold	Francis Amyot	*Canadian Singles Canoeing*
Silver	John Loaring	*400 m Hurdles*
	Harvey Charters, Frank Saker	*Canadian Pairs*
	Canadian Basketball Team	*Basketball*

Bronze   Philip Edwards   *800 m*
          Elizabeth Taylor   *80 m Hurdles*
          Women's Relay Team   *400 m Relay*
          Joseph Schleimer   *Middleweight Wrestling*
          Harvey Charters, Frank Saker   *1000 m Canoeing Doubles*

1948 London
Silver   D. Bennett   *Canadian Singles*
Bronze   Women's Relay Team   *400 m Relay*
          N. Lane   *10 000 m Canoeing Singles*

1952 Helsinki
Gold   George Genereux   *Trapshooting*
Silver   Gerald Gratton   *Middleweight Weightlifting*
          D. Hawgood, K. Lane   *10 000 m Canoeing Doubles*

1956 Melbourne
Gold   Gerald Ouellette   *Small-Bore Rifle (Prone)*
          University of British Columbia   *Coxswainless Fours*
Silver   University of British Columbia   *Eights*
Bronze   Gil Boa   *Small-Bore Rifle (Prone)*
          Irene MacDonald   *Springboard Diving*
          Equestrian Team   *Three-Day Event*

1960 Rome
Silver   University of British Columbia   *Eights*

1964 Tokyo
Gold   George Hungerford, Roger Jackson   *Coxswainless Pairs*
Silver   William Crothers   *800 m*
          Douglas Rogers   *Heavyweight Judo*
Bronze   Harry Jerome   *100 m*

1968 Mexico
Gold   Equestrian Team   *Grand Prix (Jumping)*
Silver   Elaine Tanner   *100 m Backstroke*
          Elaine Tanner   *200 m Backstroke*
          Ralph Hutton   *400 m Free Style*
Bronze   Women's Swim Team   *400 m Free Style Relay*

1972 Munich
Silver   Leslie Cliff   *400 m Individual Medley*
          Bruce Robertson   *100 m Butterfly*
Bronze   Donna Marie Gurr   *200 m Backstroke*
          Men's Swim Team   *400 m Relay*
          Yachting Team   *Soling Class*

Further Reading

Batemen, Robert, *The Book of the Olympic Game.* London: Stanley, Paul and Co. Ltd., 1968.

Batten, Jack, *Champions: Great Figures in Canadian Sport.* Toronto: New Press, 1971.

Binfield, R. D., *The Story of the Olympic Games.* London: Oxford University Press, 1948.

Carroll, Jock, *The Summer Olympic Games.* Toronto: Simon and Schuster, 1972.

Chester, David, *The Olympic Games Handbook.* Winnipeg: Greywood Publishing Ltd., 1968.

Coote, James, *A Picture History of the Olympics.* New York: The Macmillan Co., 1972.

Frayne, Trent and Peter Gzowski, *Great Canadian Sports Stories.* Toronto: Canadian

Centennial Publishing Co., 1965.

Harris, H. A., *Greek Athletes and Athletics.* London: Hutchinson of London, 1964.

———, *Sport in Greece and Rome.* London: Thames and Hudson, 1972.

Howel, Nancy and Maxwell, *Sport and Games in Canadian Life – 1700 to the Present.* Toronto: The Macmillan Co. of Canada, 1969.

Kiernan, John and Arthur Daley, *The Story of the Olympic Games.* New York: J. B. Lippincott Co., 1972.

Mandell, Richard D., *The Nazi Olympics.* New York: The Macmillan Co., 1971.

Poole, Lynn and Gray, *History of Ancient Olympic Games.* New York: Ivan Obolensky Inc., 1963.

Report of the Task Force on Sports for Canadians. Ottawa: Queen's Printer, 1969.

Roxborough, Henry, *Canada at the Olympics.* Toronto: Ryerson Press, 1963.

———, *Great Days in Canadian Sport.* Toronto: Ryerson Press, 1957.

———, *One Hundred Not Out – The Story of Nineteenth Century Canadian Sport.* Toronto: Ryerson Press, 1966.

Schaap, Richard, *An Illustrated History of the Olympics.* New York: Alfred A. Knopf, 1963.

Wise, S. F. and Douglas Fisher, *Canada's Sporting Heroes.* Don Mills: General Publishing Co., 1974.

The Book

There are people in Canada who are unquestionably special; people who continually fight the public's indifference, the government's bureaucracy and their own limits of stamina and dedication.

They are Canada's Olympic Gold Medallists.

Olympic Gold tells the stories of all of Canada's Gold Medallists since the first medal was won by the Winnipeg Shamrocks Lacrosse Club in 1904; stories of individual struggles, long lonely hours of practice with makeshift and borrowed equipment, agonizing self-sacrifice and incredible determination, all centred towards one goal: To enter, alone and unsupported, the most demanding athletic competitions in the world, and win.

Among these remarkable people are:

Etienne Desmarteau—Canada's first individual Gold Medallist, he had to quit his job as a Montreal Policeman because his superiors wouldn't give him time off to go to the Olympics.

Billy Sherring—Hamilton wouldn't give him the money to go to Athens so he risked everything he had on a horserace. His horse won the race and he won the Olympic Marathon.

Ethel Catherwood and the "Matchless Six"—Even the Pope didn't want women in the Olympics, but when public pressure finally won out, it was Canada's "Saskatoon Lily" and the women's track and field team who were first.

Francis Amyot—The Canadian Team didn't want him so he made his own way from Ottawa to the "Nazi Olympics" where he became the only Canadian Gold Medallist of 1936.

George Genereux—Plagued by mumps and algebra, George persevered and became Canada's youngest Gold Medallist.

Hungerford and Jackson—It takes years for a paired rowing team to work successfully together and get up to world class competition. For these two students from the University of British Columbia, it took six weeks.

Also included are over a hundred photographs and illustrations, some dating back to Canada's first Olympic participation in 1904, and a complete chart showing all of Canada's Olympic Medallists—Gold, Silver and Bronze.

The Authors

Frank Cosentino

Frank Cosentino, for ten years a quarterback in the CFL, used his background with great success when he began coaching the University of Western Ontario Mustangs. With his considerable experience and skill as a coach, Dr. Cosentino led the Mustangs to two national championships, after which he began to concentrate on teaching and writing about Canada's sports' history.

He is the author and coauthor of two other books about Canada's sports' heritage and his work today focuses on Canada's role in the Olympics.

Glynn Leyshon

Glynn Leyshon is an accomplished athlete, coach and writer.

He has coached Canadian wrestlers at numerous international events in such countries as the USSR, USA, Iran and Cuba.

As assistant Dean of the Faculty of Education at the University of Western Ontario, Dr. Leyshon teaches Anatomy and, as coach of the University's champion wrestling team, was named the Canadian wrestling "Coach of the Year" for 1974-75.

Both Drs. Cosentino and Leyshon were born and raised in Hamilton, Ontario, a city with a strong sports' heritage and home of two of Canada's Olympic Gold Medallists: Billy Sherring and Bobby Kerr.